Library of
Davidson College

BUCKNELL REVIEW

*Comedias del Siglo de Oro* and Shakespeare

STATEMENT OF POLICY

BUCKNELL REVIEW is a scholarly interdisciplinary journal. Each issue is devoted to a major theme or movement in the humanities or sciences, or to two or three closely related topics. The editors invite heterodox, orthodox, and speculative ideas and welcome manuscripts from any enterprising scholar in the humanities and sciences.

This journal is a member of the Conference of Editors of Learned Journals

BUCKNELL REVIEW
*A Scholarly Journal of Letters, Arts, and Sciences*

*Editors*
RICHARD FLEMING
MICHAEL PAYNE

*Associate Editor*
DOROTHY L. BAUMWOLL

*Assistant Editor*
STEVEN W. STYERS

*Editorial Board*
PATRICK BRADY
WILLIAM E. CAIN
JAMES M. HEATH
STEVEN MAILLOUX
JOHN WHEATCROFT

Contributors should send manuscripts with a self-addressed stamped envelope to the Editors, Bucknell University, Lewisburg, Pennsylvania, 17837.

BUCKNELL REVIEW

*Comedias del Siglo de Oro* and Shakespeare

Edited by
SUSAN L. FISCHER

LEWISBURG
BUCKNELL UNIVERSITY PRESS
LONDON AND TORONTO: ASSOCIATED UNIVERSITY PRESSES

© 1989 by Associated University Presses, Inc.

Associated University Presses
440 Forsgate Drive
Cranbury, NJ 08512

Associated University Presses
25 Sicilian Avenue
London WC1A 2QH, England

Associated University Presses
P.O. Box 488, Port Credit
Mississauga, Ontario
Canada L5G 4M2

The paper used in this publication meets the requirements of the American National Standard for Permanence of Paper for Printed Library Materials Z39.48-1984.

**Library of Congress Cataloging in Publication Data**

Comedias del siglo de oro and Shakespeare.

   Bucknell review ; v. 33, no. 1)
   Includes bibliographies.
   1. Shakespeare, William, 1564–1616—Criticism and interpretation.  2. Shakespeare, William, 1564–1616—Comedies.  3. Spanish drama—Classical period, 1500–1700—History and criticism.  4. Spanish drama (Comedy)—History and criticism.  5. Literature, Comparative—English and Spanish.  6. Literature, Comparative—Spanish and English.  7. Comedy.  I. Fischer, Susan L. II. Series.
AP2.B887   vol. 33, no. 1    [822.3'3] 051 s        88-48038
[PR2976]
ISBN 0-8387-5169-5 (alk. paper)

**(Volume XXXIII, Number 1)**

PRINTED IN THE UNITED STATES OF AMERICA

# Contents

| | | |
|---|---|---|
| Notes on Contributors | | 9 |
| Foreword | BRUCE W. WARDROPPER | 11 |
| The Chev'ril Glove: The Comedies of Calderón and Shakespeare | WILLIAM R. BLUE | 19 |
| "But Not for Love": Lope's *El ganso de oro* and *As You Like It* | FREDERICK A. DE ARMAS | 35 |
| Tirso's Festive Comedy: *El vergonzoso en palacio* and *As You Like It* | SUSAN L. FISCHER | 50 |
| *Romeo and Juliet* as Tragicomedy: Lope's *Castelvines y Monteses* and Rojas Zorrilla's *Los bandos de Verona* | EDWARD H. FRIEDMAN | 82 |
| *Hamlet* and *El médico de su honra*: The Significance of Intrigue | BRUCE GOLDEN | 97 |
| Elemental Ambiguity in *El hijo del sol, Faetón* and *The Tempest* | DENISE M. DIPUCCIO | 116 |
| Translating Calderón: Some Problems | KENNETH MUIR | 132 |
| Afterword | WALTER COHEN | 142 |

Recent Issues of BUCKNELL REVIEW

*Phenomenology, Structuralism, Semiology*
*Twentieth-Century Poetry, Fiction, Theory*
*Literature and History*
*New Dimensions in the Humanities and Social Sciences*
*Women, Literature, Criticism*
*The Arts and Their Interrelations*
*Shakespeare: Contemporary Approaches*
*Romanticism, Modernism, Postmodernism*
*Theories of Reading, Looking, and Listening*
*Literature, Arts, and Religion*
*Literature and Ideology*
*Science and Literature*
*The American Renaissance: New Dimensions*
*Rhetoric, Literature, and Interpretation*
*The Arts, Society, Literature*
*Text, Interpretation, Theory*
*Perspective, Art, Literature, Participation*
*Self, Sign, and Symbol*
*Criticism, History, and Intertextuality*
*New Interpretations of American Literature*
*The Senses of Stanley Cavell*
*John Cage at Seventy-Five*

# Notes on Contributors

FREDERICK A. DE ARMAS is professor of Spanish and Comparative Literature at The Pennsylvania State University. His books include *The Invisible Mistress: Aspects of Feminism and Fantasy in the Golden Age; Critical Perspectives on Calderón de la Barca* (Co-Editor); and *The Return of Astraea: An Astral-Imperial Myth in Calderón.*

WILLIAM R. BLUE is professor of Spanish at the University of Kansas. He is author of *The Development of Imagery in Calderón's* Comedias; and Comedia: *Art and History.*

WALTER COHEN is associate professor of Comparative Literature at Cornell University. He has published *Drama of a Nation: Public Theater in Renaissance England and Spain.*

DENISE M. DIPUCCIO is associate professor of Spanish at the University of Tennessee (Knoxville). She is currently working on a book entitled *A Reevaluation of the Mythological Tradition in Golden Age Drama.*

SUSAN L. FISCHER is associate professor of Spanish at Bucknell University. Her article "Calderón's *Los cabellos de Absalón (Absalom's Locks)* and the Semiotics of Performance" recently appeared in the *Bulletin of the Comediantes.* At present, she is engaged in a study entitled *Text and Performance: Spanish Golden Age Theatre in a Modern Context.*

EDWARD H. FRIEDMAN is professor of Spanish at Arizona State University. Two of his books are *The Unifying Concept: Approaches to the Structure of Cervantes'* comedias, and *The Antiheroine's Voice: Narrative Discourse and Transformations of the Picaresque.*

BRUCE GOLDEN is professor of English at California State University, San Bernardino. He has written articles on Ford Madox Ford, Calderón, and Lope de Vega.

KENNETH MUIR is Emeritus Professor of English Literature at Liverpool University and Vice-President of the International Shakespeare Association. He has made thirteen verse translations of plays by Racine, Corneille, and Calderón, five of which have been performed.

BRUCE W. WARDROPPER is William Hane Wannamaker Professor of Romance Languages at Duke University. Among his books are *Teatro español del Siglo de Oro; Critical Essays on the Theatre of Calderón; Spanish Poetry of the Golden Age;* and a translation and edition, with an introduction and commentary, of Calderón's *El mágico prodigioso (The Prodigious Magician)*.

# Foreword

Bruce W. Wardropper
*Duke University*

THE reader of the *Bucknell Review* has every reason to wonder why a whole issue has been devoted to comparative studies of Shakespeare and Spanish dramatists of the seventeenth century. Some thoughtful possible answers to this question are given by Walter Cohen in his Afterword. Cohen notes formal dramatic similarities, autonomously reached by playwrights in England and Spain, which invite speculation and comparison. He also mentions the probable desire of the participating critics, most of whom are Hispanists, "to promote their area of professional specialization." The extraordinary quantitative florescence of drama under the Spanish Habsburgs has indeed been strangely neglected by cultivated readers and theatergoers in the United States. If this issue of the *Bucknell Review* piques readers' curiosity about Spanish baroque drama, it will have accomplished at least one beneficial purpose.

Some guideposts to Spanish baroque drama may be helpful to the general reader. The Spanish drama of this period is collectively referred to as the *comedia,* and individual plays are referred to as *comedias.* The *comedia* was created, and imposed on the Spanish stage, by Lope de Vega, a commoner who lived from 1562 to 1635. He created it more by example than by precept. Over four hundred extant plays by Lope exemplify the *comedia.* All are in verse, and in a wide variety of metrical forms, both Spanish and Italian. Each of the three—not five—acts contains approximately one thousand lines of verse. Each play was written for an acting company, which by tradition had actors specializing in playing an old man, two or three dashing gallants, and a fool, the *gracioso,* and actresses—not boys—who played leading ladies, ingénues, and maidservants. Despite their specializations, the actors and actresses were versatile, and could tackle plays with the most diverse characters and plots. Although strictly speaking *comedia* means comedy, and most *comedias* end happily, many of the plays were tragicomedies and some, tragedies. The plots varied greatly. Among others, there were plays about the life of peasants in fiefdoms, religious plays, chronicle plays, romantic comedies, and even mythological plays, although these were mainly written for the court theater.

The popular theaters were called *corrales* because they originated in the rectangular space enclosed by the walls of blocks of houses. In such *corrales* plays were first performed in Madrid in the late 1560s. The stage at first had only the most rudimentary props. The place and changes of scene were conveyed by the dialogue. Theatrical conditions were, then, roughly similar in London and Madrid.

Lope de Vega had numerous followers, both contemporaries and successors. I shall mention only those whose plays are discussed in this issue of the *Bucknell Review*. Lope's most notable contemporary playwright was Friar Gabriel Téllez (1584?–1648), who wrote plays under the pseudonym Tirso de Molina. Tirso, a great admirer of Lope's dramaturgy, paid him the tribute of closely following his model. In his plays (a small part of his literary production), Cervantes (1547–1616) rejected Lope's model, and, as a consequence, was rebuffed, at least in his later years, by the producers of drama. Today we admire particularly his one-act farces in prose, which are called *entremeses,* or interludes.

Don Pedro Calderón de la Barca (1600–1681), an aristocrat, essentially followed Lope's lead, but he altered the paradigm in several distinctive ways. He reduced the variety of metrical forms in his plays, much preferring native Spanish ones. At the same time he used a more elevated level of poetic discourse based on a more complex system of poetic imagery. He adjusted his plays to the more sophisticated stage machinery that was available to him. After his ordination in 1651, he wrote only mythological plays and romantic comedies for the court and one-act allegorical plays for the public celebration of the Feast of Corpus Christi. Francisco de Rojas Zorrilla (1607–1648) is generally considered a member of Calderón's second phase of *comedia* writing. By 1650 the popular drama had passed its heyday, though reruns and fresh adaptations of *comedias* occupied public theaters through the eighteenth century.

In his revolutionary book *Drama of a Nation: Public Theater in Renaissance England and Spain* (1985), Walter Cohen makes the point that, while French drama is that of a social class, English and Spanish drama, equally that of a class, "is also the drama of a nation" (p. 150). Notwithstanding "the absence of capitalism and radical Protestantism" (p. 260) in Spain, the two countries both achieved nationhood in the seventeenth century. Similar social and political currents—among them, the adaptation of the aristocracy to the drive toward absolutism—conspired to produce a formal kinship in the public drama of both countries. To explore this kinship Cohen adopts an approach which approximates both Louis Althusser's "symptomatic reading" and Fredric Jameson's "metacommentary." "Symptomatic reading seeks to show the systematic relation between presences and absences, between the visible and the invisible, between what is said and what cannot be said within any problematic, any genre, or any play. Metacommentary's purpose is not merely to arrive at an interpretation, but also to interrogate interpretation itself, to ask why it is needed at all and to determine what its response to the text or performance of a play reveals or, more importantly, obscures" (p. 186). Cohen carries off this radically new enterprise in the field of *comedia* studies with brilliant ingenuity, illuminating in a new way not only the processes that shaped Spanish and English drama independently into similar molds but also the generic structures of this drama of two nations. But it is no slight to his accomplishment to say that his book remains controversial. It remains true that other means of comparing the two dramaturgies are viable.

The authors of the essays in this number of the *Bucknell Review* were, I suspect, subjected to massive training in formalist criticism in their graduate schools. It is not, I think, Cohen's "settling of accounts with the prior generation of critics of the *comedia*" that motivated the writing of these essays. Rather it is a search for some new methodology that would be congenial to critics habituated to doing close reading of texts. Various kinds of post-structuralism, with their emphasis on the evanescence and inaccessibility of written texts, seem unsatisfactory to many would-be post-formalists. What we have in these essays is an attempt to supersede the past without embracing a present that at times seems chaotic. The essays are at once interpretations and a search for a method of criticism.

One of the problems that American Hispanists face (apart from the culture's privileging of English, French, and German literature) is that the first literature seriously studied by many of them has been in Spanish. They have thus inherited the "belatedness" of Spanish culture and of Hispanic studies that even so eminent a Spanish scholar as Ramón Menéndez Pidal acknowledged. Few Hispanists have studied in depth the work of the Elizabethan and Jacobean playwrights. But in high school and college it was not easy for them to avoid reading through a play or two by Shakespeare. Justly or unjustly, our tradition and our culture have made Shakespeare the bench mark of English dramatic literature and the greatest manipulator of the English language.

Shakespeare's extraordinary impact on the high and low cultures of English speakers is undeniable. Aphorisms from his works have become commonplaces of civilized discourse: "The better part of valor is discretion"; "The world's mine oyster"; "Brevity is the soul of wit." Less recognized perhaps is the extent to which spoken English, even among the less educated, is impregnated with Shakespearean idiom: "laid on with a trowel"; "cold comfort"; "salad days"; "at one fell swoop"; "eaten me out of house and home"; "sink or swim." Far more than that of, say, Marlowe or Jonson, Shakespeare's language has shaped the way we speak and write. Like it or not, Shakespeare forms a part of the expressiveness of those whose native language is English.

Furthermore, the high esteem in which Shakespeare's plays were held by his contemporaries, and have continued to be held by succeeding generations and centuries, has turned this writer into an Anglophone monument on a par with Cervantes in Spain and Goethe in Germany. It is hard not to use Shakespeare's works as a springboard to a better understanding of the *comedia;* and it is hard not to use Shakespearean criticism in its not quite infinite variety as models to be tested on Spanish plays. Invigorated by Shakespearean texts and studies, the essays collected here make a considerable contribution both to *comedia* studies and to the comparative study of Shakespeare and Spanish baroque dramatists.

In his Afterword, Walter Cohen proposes as a future critical enterprise a reversal of the terms of comparison used in these essays, bringing *comedia* studies to bear on Shakespeare's drama. "The aim here would be to defamiliarize Shakespeare's plays by placing them in what remains a largely alien context in this country." I subscribe to this program. An earnest example of how fruitful it might be is an essay written over thirty-five years ago by Edward M. Wilson, which remained unpublished in its complete form until it appeared posthumously in his book *Spanish and English Literature of the Sixteenth and Seventeenth Centuries* (1980). Entitled "A Hispanist Looks at *Othello,*" the essay considers the tragedy in the light of the Spanish code of honor, which, far from being exclusively Spanish, is nevertheless displayed with casuistic punctiliousness in Spanish drama. Wilson intended "to show: 1. how the idea of honour binds the play together, and 2. that Shakespeare was also concerned with the importance of the cardinal virtues (prudence, justice, temperance and fortitude) and the evils of rashness, cunning and injustice" (p. 203). In this undertaking, as in all to which he set his hand, Wilson was eminently successful. Although his social and political values were different from Cohen's, in this essay Wilson laid the foundation for Cohen's program. His essay may well serve as complementary reading for the readers of this splendid collection of essays on Shakespeare and the *comedia*.

BUCKNELL REVIEW

*Comedias del Siglo de Oro* and Shakespeare

# The Chev'ril Glove: The Comedies of Calderón and Shakespeare

William R. Blue
*University of Kansas*

BOTH Shakespearean and Spanish Golden Age comedy participate in the festival and carnival spirit. C. L. Barber links the English dramatist's comedies to Elizabethan holidays, to "morris-dances, sword dances, wassailings, mock ceremonies of summer kings and queens and of lords of misrule, mummings, disguisings, masques . . . Candlemas, Shrove Tuesday, Hocktide, May Day, Whitsuntide, Midsummer Eve, Harvest-home, Halloween, and the twelve days of the Christmas season ending with Twelfth Night."[1] Similar festivities abounded in Spain during the Habsburg reign:

> In January, Circumcision, Epiphany [Twelfth Night]; in February, Purification and Saint Matthew; in March, Saint Joseph and the Annunciation; in May, Saint Philip and Saint James the Lesser—known in Madrid as Saint James the Green. . . . The feast and merriment days accumulated throughout the century with the birth of new members of the Royal Family, whose birth and Saint's Days were celebrated, along with their baptisms, weddings . . . [as were] commemorations of battles and victories, along with the entrances and exits of the King and court.[2]

Many of these events called for new plays to be written and performed before the royal family and/or in public theaters.

It has been far too easy for many critics to dismiss comedy and carnival as momentary misrule, as an unimportant parenthesis of joy and laughter, of foolish topsy-turviness, in a long, serious sentence. Yet Bruce Wardropper has argued for a deeper understanding of both comedy and festival:

> The festivals (Carnival in particular) are the institution by which society sanctions antisocial behaviour under preestablished and transitory conditions. . . . Comedy, the theatrical expression of that antisocial psychic energy, has its origins in festive celebrations and the courting customs of the young.[3]

Mikhail Bakhtin has written extensively on carnival's subversiveness. Folk humor, the carnivalesque, Bakhtin asserts, offered a positive alternative to the formal, oppressive power structure: a possibility of liberation from the present order of life, a belief in change, in becoming, in the brief triumph of the people over received ideology.[4]

In Spain in the seventeenth century, as in England in the sixteenth and seventeenth, old structures are breaking down, but the new forms (of economics, sociology, politics, etc.) have not yet taken a completely recognizable, concrete form. This is an age of transition, of doubt and faith, of unstable stability, of a desire to shake off the known harnessed by a fear of the unknown. Some of these tensions are reflected in the comedies of this period, and the laughter these plays produce is ambiguous. Comedy, like carnival, seems to offer up alternatives and then back away from them, but the possibilities, along with the doubts, fears, questions, and criticisms raised by these plays, do not vanish when man marries woman in the last scene. It may be that if the intention of comedy is to allay suspicions about its "subversiveness" through laughter, deceit, and role-play, then embracing order in the final scene may be the ultimate joke. These plays flaunt their own conventions to such a degree that their own theatricality is the sign of an antimimesis which cannot be restrained, despite the inclusion of quotidian activities, gross materiality, and local references. In their carnivalesque playfulness with language, identity, and self-reflexivity lies their contrariness to the status quo.

In the comedies, language is pushed toward its limits of rhetorical pomp—in the lovers' speeches—on the one hand, and of punning madness—usually by the *gracioso* or fool—on the other. I have no doubt that Shakespeare is a more constant and outrageous punster than his Spanish counterparts, though the latter do have their moments. But Shakespeare mounts a frontal attack on language itself, for example, in the personage of the Clown in *Twelfth Night:*

> To see this age! A sentence is but a chev'ril glove to a good wit. How quickly the wrong side may be turned outward! . . . Troth sir, I can yield you none [reason] without words, and words are grown so false I am loath to prove reason with them.
> [3.1. 11–13, 23–25]

A good wit can turn a sentence, reason, and the world inside out. If words are false, reason is false for there can now be no reason with or without words because words are without reason; language has become unhitched from reality and, like Don Quixote, language wanders off creating a life of its own on the margins of reality. What is at stake in this situation is order itself. An ordered society depends on a strong connection between words and things, words and concepts, words and laws for its stability. What comedy questions, inverts, and destabilizes with its word play, with words "grown so false," is the ordered state itself. Terry Eagleton expands upon this notion and observes about Shakespeare what we could also see in Tirso de Molina or Calderón de la Barca: Shakespeare's "belief in social stability is jeopardized by the very [punning, troping, riddling] language in which it is articulated."[5]

As Wardropper has clearly shown, Spanish Golden Age dramatists exploit language as well. Though there may not be the kind of direct assault by someone like the Clown, the effect is the same. In his discussion of Lope de Vega's *Sembrar en buena tierra (To Sow on Good Ground)*, a young gallant follows and yet inverts his father's sound advice—spend your money with prudence (gastar con prudencia)—by relying on a pun. The object of the young man's affections is a money-hungry shrew on whom Félix showers gifts. He drops his qualms about spending large amounts on her because her name is Prudence.[6]

In Tirso de Molina's *El vergonzoso en palacio (The Bashful Man in the Palace)*,[7] the *gracioso*'s word play leans heavily on the scatalogical. In the following passage, he manages to conflate the scatalogical and the religious realms in a series of outrageous puns, of which my translation must inevitably be awkward (puns are indicated by slashes):

¡Santos estrellados!
Doléos de quien de miedo está en tortilla;
y, si hay algún devoto de lacayos,
sáqueme de este aprieto, y yo le juro
de colgalle mis calzas a la puerta
de su templo, en lavándolas diez veces
y limpiando la cera de sus barrios;
que, aunque las enceró mi pena fiera,
no es buena para ofrendas esta cera.

[1. 497–505]

Starry Saints!/Holy fried eggs!
Have pity on him who from fear is in a fix/omlette
and if there is any saint for servants,
let him get me out of this jam, and I swear to him
that I will hang my pants [as an offering] on the door
of his temple, after washing them ten times
and cleaning the wax/excrement from their confines;
for although my fierce suffering/shame waxed/soiled them,
this wax/excrement is no good as an offering/votive candle.

The word unhinged, the conflation of the divine and the dirty reflects other discontinuities and bizarre conjoinings afoot in this time, as well as the carnivalesque overturning of the norm.

The crisis in representation resonates throughout the comedies not only in language but also in the constant use of masking, disguising, and role-playing. To achieve the happy end of their unleashed desires, characters in the comedies, like their language, run riot. The Duke in *Twelfth Night* slides verbally from love to music to food to gluttony to death in only three lines:

> If music be the food of love, play on.
> Give me the excess of it, that, surfeiting,
> The appetite may sicken, and so die.
>
> [1.1.1–3]

Likewise Viola, actually a boy playing a woman, adopts the guise of a man, actually a eunuch, to serve the Duke with the intent of turning his desire for the fair Olivia to Viola herself.

In *A Midsummer Night's Dream,* the characters need neither disguise nor mistaken identity for riotous error to occur since Shakespeare has the mischievous Puck "accidentally" pull the wrong strings thereby creating confusion and disaffection among the puppetlike lovers. Similarly, in Tirso de Molina's most complicated love comedy, *Don Gil de las calzas verdes (Don Gil of the Green Tights),* the jilted, abandoned Doña Juana puckishly makes all the other characters dance to her brightly played tune. Like Puck, she can apparently assume whatever form she pleases at a moment's notice.

Unlike *A Midsummer Night's Dream,* the bulk of which takes place in the woods near Athens, the common setting for most seventeenth-century Spanish comedies is Madrid. These are urban comedies that make exact reference to the streets, buildings, and areas in Spain's principal city. Wardropper has observed that there "the lovers embark on an unrealizable search, the illogical search for Arcadia in the heart of the capital" (Los enamorados se embarcan en una búsqueda irrealizable, la ilógica búsqueda de la Arcadia en el corazón de la capital).[8] Madrid was haphazardly built, with labyrinthical, often filthy streets, hot in the summer, cold in winter, overcrowded, teeming with unsavory characters, but it was the seat of power, the home of the king and his court, the political land of promise, opportunity, dreams, successes, and failures.

There, for the greater part of the seventeenth century, Philip IV ruled, and if there was ever a king who knew what theater and the theatrical was, it was he. Under the directorship of the Count-Duke Olivares, emerged the public character Philip would play. The notion of Olivares as director, Philip as actor, is not far-fetched. J. H. Elliott's description of Olivares molding Philip is clearly akin to an older, confident director bringing along a young actor with great potential but little formal training:

> He [Olivares] had observed in him [Philip] a quick wit and a natural intelligence. Philip had also proved to be a good athlete and horseman, and his bearing and manner were potentially those of a king. But both mentally and emotionally he lacked discipline, and his education had in many respects been hopelessly inadequate. A few days from his sixteenth birthday at the time of his accession, he was, however, still young enough to be trained and moulded to conform to the ideal image of a King of Spain. . . . By persuading Philip that kingship was an art that had to learned, and by offering to guide his first hesitant steps, Olivares helped to counter his [Philip's] deep sense of inadequacy.[9]

Moreover Philip was an avid theater goer and even performed in certain palace plays and masques. Yet as Elliott hints, behind the cultured, imposing mask of king cowered the self-doubting, self-indulgent man. His amorous indulgences provided grist for Madrid's ever-present gossip mills; his confessional letters to Sor Agreda provide insight into his self-recriminations; and yet the face he showed to the public was stern, even severe. In public, Philip was a terrific actor. Fiction is latent in reality; politics and power, as Eagleton states, are histrionic. "Society itself," he continues, "is a dramatic artefact, demanding a certain suspension of disbelief on the part of its members. . . . There is no social reality without its admixture of feigning, mask, performance, delusion, just as there is no sign which cannot be used to deceive. Being yourself always involves a degree of play-acting."[10]

"All the world's a stage," declares Shakespeare; Calderón speaks of *el gran teatro del mundo*. Masks, façade, purchased titles of nobility, men of noble birth dressing well but living on less than a shoestring, healthy men posing as crippled beggars to make ends meet, priests with lovers: theater was more than a metaphor, it was a way of life. It is no wonder that, as in life, in the plays characters can slip from role to role at will.

In one of Calderón de la Barca's most complicated comedies, *Mañana será otro día (Tomorrow Is Another Day)*,[11] the heroine, Beatriz, takes or has thrust upon her five roles. The causes for her protean shifts are the usual: intentional deceit in the name of love and mistaken identity brought about by being in the wrong place at the wrong time. She is mistaken for her brother Juan's sweetheart; she is Fernando's contracted wife-to-be; she is the "wanton" sister; and she invents two roles, the Countess and Brianda de Bentivolli. In this play, Calderón himself is the ironic Puck who squeezes the juice from the "love-in-idleness" on the eyelids of his characters, and he goes out of his way to invite his knowing audience to watch him perform his magic.

Since this is not one of the playwright's best-known comedies, I am going to give a brief plot summary.

Don Luis de Ayala has two children, Don Juan and Beatriz. She is promised in marriage to a man she has never seen, Don Fernando. Don Juan, recently returned from the army, angered his father and was thrown out of the house. Subsequently, Juan filed suit against his father for the inheritance due him through his deceased mother and, moreover, has taken her last name, Leyva, as his. Juan is currently courting two women, Elvira and Leonor. His companion is a worldy man called Capitán.

One night outside Elvira's house, Juan is attacked by another of Elvira's suitors, but since a crowd gathers, the two men withdraw. Elvira, ignorant of the familial relationship, seeks Beatriz's reluctant aid to assuage Juan's anger. The two ladies to go Leonor's house to change clothes so as to avoid any possible recognition. At the meeting, Juan and the Captain are attacked by the other suitor and his friend, and Juan wounds his rival. Beatriz escapes unrecognized with the aid of an unknown noble who turns out to be Fernando. She goes to Leonor's house to change clothes, but Juan has previously arrived there to speak with Leonor. He recognizes his sister, pulls his dagger to kill her thinking that she is playing fast and loose with the family honor. Leonor, thinking that the woman is Elvira, prevents Juan from acting, jealously berates him, and thus gives Beatriz time to escape. On the way home, she seeks protection from a nobleman she sees on the street, and once more he turns out to be Fernando.

Leonor, Fernando's cousin, after realizing that the unknown woman was not Elvira, tries to find out who she was. Fernando goes to Luis's house and, though he does not recognize Beatriz, she does know him and she is thrilled. Fernando is taken with her, but later, when Leonor tells him about a certain flirty woman named Beatriz, he begins to devise a way out of the potentially dangerous marriage. Before he can leave, he receives two mysterious notes from unknown women begging him not to depart.

Beatriz, having decided to win Fernando at all costs, sends both notes. She leads Fernando through a merry and mystifying evening, which ends with the young man being accused by three different women of toying with their affections. Luis and Juan are about to attack the thoroughly confused gallant when Beatriz steps forward, explains the mysteries, and accepts Fernando's hand in marriage. Juan pledges his troth to Elvira at the same moment.

As I mentioned earlier, throughout the play as characters slide from role to role, from one confusing and often dangerous situation to the next, the dramatist invites the spectators to see "what fools these mortals be," to distance themselves and watch "their fond pageant." Since there is no Puck in this play, Calderón uses other means to invite a certain disengagement. The first might be the all too frequent fortuitous circumstance: the unknown gallant who just happens along when Beatriz is in trouble, who saves her twice, who is noble and handsome, and who just happens to be the very man to whom her father has promised her in marriage. The chances of that happening in the hustle and bustle of Madrid are so remote that the spectator cannot but smile at the manipulating hand of the dramatist who, like a magician, winks slyly as he shows us "there's nothing up my sleeve."

The playwright uses self-conscious intertextuality as well to achieve similar effects. That is to say, he insists on telling us time and again that this is fiction. When, for example, against Roque's advice, Fernando first leaps to Beatriz's aid, the servant creates a verb that for him synthesizes his master's ridiculous chivalry: "My master has become Quixotified" (Enquijotóse mi amo, p. 756b). Roque follows up his own verbal lead in act 2 declaring Fernando's chivalrous persona a "borrowed Don Quixote" (Don Quijote de prestado) and a "small-time Don Esplandián" (Don Esplandián de poquito, p. 774a).[12] By such references, Roque emphasizes Fernando's anachronistic, cartoonlike comportment, stresses the outrageous lengths a nobleman might go to for a woman, and marks the vast gap between his pragmatic, self-serving viewpoint and his master's overblown sense of gallantry.

Furthermore, Calderón scatters numerous references to his own earlier comedies throughout *Mañana será otro día*. Juana thinks it should be easy for Fernando to discover that Beatriz has brought him to her house at night through a second door that opens onto a side street: "Would it be so difficult to discover that this house has two doors?" (¿Tan dificultoso ha sido / saber que en esta casa hay dos puertas?, p. 775b). In 1629, Calderón wrote a popular play called *Casa con dos puertas (The House with Two Doors)* in which the same architectural feature was the basis for confusion. The two mysterious notes Beatriz sends Fernando are signed La Dama de la Justicia and La Dama de Cienvinos and thereby harken back to another note-writing mysterious lady in love in *La dama duende (The Phantom Lady),* also from 1629. Roque likens his master's steadily deteriorating plight to yet another play: "I hope this is not the comedy from Bad to Worse" [No sea esta comedia / de peor está que estaba, p. 798b).

Beatriz, from a more general perspective, likens her own role-playing to theater: "and so I must double my role in this love farce, being one person playing three roles" (y así, / he de doblar mi papel / con esta farsa de amor, / siendo una, y haciendo tres, p. 784a). In these roles she both acts and directs as she tries to orchestrate the last scenes to come out as she desires. But perhaps the most brazen instance of self-reflexivity occurs at the very end. After the young lovers have paired off, it is traditional in Spanish Golden Age comedies for the *gracioso* to step forward with some final joke or quibble and ask the audience for applause. In this play, Roque not only does that but he ties up all the loose ends that the dramatist apparently "forgot":

> Esperen vuesas mercedes,
> que decir tres cosas falta.
> Ya se acordarán que hubo
> en la primera jornada
> un don Diego, y que le dieron
> en ella una cuchillada
> él se la ha estado curando,
> y por eso de aquí falta.
> También hubo una Leonor
> introducida en la farsa,
> y no está aquí, porque fuera
> malo el salir de su casa
> a estas horas de estos dos
> cuentan mil historias largas
> que se casaron. También
> se acuerdan que entró en la danza
> una maleta perdida:
> desta sola no se halla
> tradición. Aquesto he dicho
> porque no me queda nada
> que decir: si vuesarcedes
> de la comedia se agradan,
> <<mañana será otro día>>,
> para que vengan a honrarla.
>
> [P. 799b]

> Wait, ladies and gentlemen,
> three things are yet to be said.

> You will remember that there was
> in the first act
> one Don Diego, and that in that act
> he was stabbed with a sword.
> Well, he's still recuperating
> and that's why he's not here right now.
> Also there was a Leonor
> introduced in this farce.
> She's not here now because it's not
> proper for her to go out of her house
> at this time of night. About these two people
> a thousand long stories are told
> about how they got married. Also
> you will remember that a lost suitcase
> of mine was a part of this story;
> about that alone can no follow up
> story be found. I have said all this
> and now there is nothing more to be
> said. If you ladies and gentlemen
> are pleased by the comedy,
> *Tomorrow Is Another Day,*
> you can now praise it.

A few years ago, the critical catchword for these self-reflexive moments was "meta-theater." But today, Malcolm Evans, among others, challenges the term: "Contrary to the opinion fashionable in the 1960s and early 1970s, there is no 'meta-language' or 'meta-drama' in the comedies, no level of representation which can fix 'what is *really* going on,' only more production, more text."[13] Whereas the "Yale-variety" deconstructionists, after signaling such a *mise en abîme*, might then point to language's inability to do more than say yes and no at the same time, to talk about itself, to emphasize its own failures, "like some barroom bore,"[14] Evans follows a more productive path. He links self-reflexivity and linguistic play in the comedies to a "late sixteenth- and early seventeenth-century crisis in representation." He ties this to Foucault's observation that this period is "the privileged age of the *trompe l'oeil* painting, of comic illusion, of the play that duplicates itself by presenting another play, of the *quid pro quo*, of dreams and visions."[15] Furthermore, what goes on in the play is a reflection of what goes on outside the theater, outside the world of art. From the king down, this is a society built on role-playing; thus the frontiers between theater and the world are most fuzzy. In this world, as in this play, the role, the disguise, the facade have begun to take the place of "the real." The supplement rules.

In the process of showing the theatricality of it all, the carnivalesque, laughing, debunking voice of the people can be heard.

In *Mañana será otro día,* that voice speaks in two differently modulated tones: in the traditionally self-serving, mercenary, gluttonous pitch of the *gracioso* Roque, and in the pragmatic, worldwise, nonchalant timber of the Captain. Roque's hunger is constant. To cite only one example, he does not want to leave Luis's house for Leonor's house as hastily as Fernando does. The return trip can wait, he avows, at least until after lunch at Luis's:

> *Roq.*                   Pero mira,
> que nos vamos sin comer,
> y en casa de tu prima
> ya habrán comido.
> *Fer.*                   ¿Qué importa?
> *Roq.* Ser lo del perro de Olías,
> que por hallarse en dos bodas,
> fué a Cabañas con gran prisa,
> y en llegando habían comido,
> y volviéndose a su villa,
> habían comido también.
> Comamos pues.
> *Fer.*                   ¡Qué porfía
> tan de hombre bajo!
> *Roq.*                   Los reyes
> son altos y comen.
>
>                                                           [P. 783a]

> *Roq.*                   But look,
> we're leaving without eating,
> and at your cousin's house
> they may have already eaten.
> *Fer.*                   What difference does that make?
> *Roq.* Let's not be like Olías's dog
> who to attend two wedding feasts
> went quickly to Cabañas
> where he found they had already eaten,
> so he returned to his own village
> and there, they had finished eating too.
> Let's eat now.
> *Fer.* That's the insistence of a low-born man!
> *Roq.* Kings are high-born, and they eat.

Furthermore, Roque is cowardly. When he and Fernando are alone in the dark room awaiting the appearance of the Countess, Roque immediately reaches for his Rosary: "when in danger I always recollect the saints" (En los riesgos / me acuerdo yo de los santos, p. 793a). In addition, he is greedy. Early on in the play, Roque loses his suitcases in which he had stashed all the money he had managed to filch from his master during their journey to Madrid. He bemoans his lost suitcase right up to the last scene.

At another point, he receives a jewel from Beatriz, in one of her many disguises, only to have another lady, Beatriz again, take it away. As he wails over his loss, Beatriz, as the Countess, gives him a gold chain. It is the perfect gift, he says, since he will now be her slave forever. Nonetheless, Roque immediately makes plans to sell it to a jeweler and he can hardly wait for day to come so he can know for sure if the chain is pure gold or not (pp. 794a/b).

While Roque falls within the traditional role of the laughable, low-class fool, he still throws several well-placed barbs into those values the nobles hold dear. As I have shown, Roque sneers at his master's chivalric actions and punningly declares that Fernando's business, apparently, is to help those in need. If he stays four more days in Madrid, there will be no more "needy people" (Amparar son sus cuidados, / y si aquí se llega a ver / cuatro días, no ha de haber / casa de desamparados, p. 769a).

Roque makes fun of the high faluting language of lovers. When Fernando sees Beatriz and discovers that she is his betrothed, it is love at first sight:

> *Fer.* ¿Sois vos su [de Luis] hija?
> (Ap. a Roque) Estoy perdido.
> *Roq.* Debes de ser mi maleta.
> *Bea.* Su hija soy.
> *Fer.* (Ap. a Roque) Hallé el sentido.
> *Roq.* Así hallara mi bolsa.
>
> [P. 775b]

> *Fer.* Are you his [Luis's] daughter?
> (Aside to Roque) I'm lost [in love].
> *Roq.* You must be my suitcase.
> *Bea.* I am his daughter.
> *Fer.* (Aside to Roque) I have found my reason.
> *Roq.* I should find my bag so easily.

After hearing the lovers exchange mutual praises in overblown language, Roque offers to kiss Beatriz's hand, imitating the very same language of supercharged metaphor:

> . . . que fuera gran disparate
> perder por inadvertido
> esta ocasión de besar
> este terso, claro y limpio
> copo de animada nieve.
>
> [P. 777a]

> . . . it would be absurd
> carelessly to lose

this opportunity to kiss
this limpid, clear, pure
flake of animated snow.

And finally, he accuses his master of being a fool for love as he thus summarizes Fernando's peripatetic, fickle behavior:

> Roque, a casarme
> voy. Roque, yo no me caso.
> Roque, al punto he de partirme.
> Roque, por hoy no me parto.
> ¡Qué hermosa, Roque, es Beatriz!
> ¡Qué ingenio tan extremado
> tiene doña Brianda, Roque!
> Roque, ¡oh qué empleo tan alto
> hoy me ofrece mi fortuna!

[P. 792b]

> Roque, I am going
> to get married. Roque, I'm not getting married.
> Roque, I have to leave right away.
> Roque, I'm not leaving.
> Roque, how beautiful is Beatriz!
> What a fantastic wit
> has Doña Brianda, Roque!
> Roque, what a noble opportunity
> my luck offers me today [with the Countess] . . .

If Roque mocks Fernando's excesses, the Captain exercises, in more measured tones, a similar function with Juan. He tells the young man that he is crazy if he believes he can court two women at the same time and not get caught (p. 761b). It is equally foolish, the Captain adds, to think you can have a sword fight in a public place and not be recognized by someone (p. 762a). In questions of honor, he counsels, prudence and time are the best measures. Acting in haste, fighting without good reason, are the marks of a precipitate fool (pp. 770a, 787b).

Roque and the Captain, the fool (servant) and the soldier, are outsiders to the nobles' value systems; both are aliens, if you will, living on the fringe of, yet living off, the order they criticize. When viewed through the lenses of Juan's and Fernando's mind set, Roque especially, and less so the Captain, are "unnatural." Yet what is natural for Juan and Fernando is the dangerously chivalrous, strutting, precipitate, jealous, fickle male alternately dominating and cowering before the woman they profess to love. In the nobleman's world, reckless sword play backs up a bizarre sense of honor—an honor code that allows single males all the excesses they wish, but denies single women an unguarded breath.

The outsiders, when joined by Beatriz and later by Elvira, create "chaos" since chaos is the only way that rigid, official society can ever imagine "the other." That "other" *is* officially sanctioned during specific but limited times of the year as the carnivalesque. In that world of the appetites, of mystery, danger, and inversion, Roque lives and Beatriz moves. There, the power structures are rendered alien and arbitrary through the invocation of carnival's power. There man and woman return to themselves.

Yet in the end, by turning the system inside out, the characters come to marriage. Marriage is that place where the individual desire, the social order, and the sacramental interlock. Though nearly all Spanish Golden Age comedies end in marriage, many of the pairings fail to satisfy us either aesthetically or emotionally. Arnold Reichenberger once said that in these plays it does not matter if a woman gets the man she wants as long as she gets a man.[16] But that simply is not true, and *Mañana será otro día* takes great pains to criticize arranged or forced marriages by fathers (or, I will add, by dramatists). The critiques, not surprisngly, are uttered by Beatriz and Roque:

> *Bea.* no me repitas mis ansias,
> pues ya sé que la mayor
> que a nadie en el mundo pasa,
> es que una mujer, por ser
> principal, de admitir haya
> esposo a elección ajena . . .
>
> [P. 773a]

> do not repeat my difficulties to me,
> since I already know that the greatest
> that can happen to anyone in the world
> is that a woman, simply by being
> of noble birth, must accept
> a husband chosen by someone else. . .

> *Roq.* La cosa que más extraño,
> de que con razón me admiro,
> es que en el mundo, señor,
> haya hombre tan atrevido
> que se case por concierto
> con quien nunca vió ni quiso.
> ¿Qué la dice a una mujer
> saber quisiera, un marido,
> que sin haberla mirado,

>             ni hablado, señor, ni escrito,
>             se entra en la cama con ella?
>
>                                              [Pp. 774b/75a]
>
>             What I find most strange,
>             what I am most surprised at,
>             sir, is that in this world
>             there can be a man so daring
>             that he gets married by arrangement
>             to someone he has never seen or loved.
>             What does a husband say
>             to a wife, I would like to know,
>             who, without ever having seen,
>             spoken to, or written her
>             he suddenly gets into bed with?

Forced marriages bother us so because they are *not* that fusion of the personal, the social, and the religious. We feel for mismatched pairs, not only for their frustrated or trampled emotions, but also because we see the oppressive hand of society falling arbitrarily on the heads of young and essentially innocent lovers.

In *Mañana será otro día*, however, Beatriz loves, and is loved by, Fernando; thus we applaud their imminent wedding. Acceptable, though not so clear-cut, is the betrothal of Juan to Elvira. Roque's efforts to drag in Leonor and Diego, however, leave much to be desired and, as he says, to be told. Roque's final narrative heightens our sense of the theatricality, the illusionary sleight of hand, of these traditional happy endings. Similarly, in *A Midsummer Night's Dream*, after all the confusion and thrashing about in the woods wherein anyone was capable of loving anyone else, the marriages strike us as high theater. There, as in Calderón's play, magic and illusion have prepared the path for the lover's reunion. What matters in the end, Eagleton says, is whether the lovers' illusions interlock. "If they do, if the illusion is total, mutual, and internally consistent, then this is perhaps the nearest we can approximate to truth or reality."[17]

In both plays, the lovers' fantastical comings and goings are capped by the sober, sacramental marriage contract with which we seem to have reached a resting place wherein personal and social reality are embraced and reorganized. But the problem is that neither Calderón nor Shakespeare stops there. Once more the dramatists turn things inside out undoing, at least partially, the reorganizing action by insisting on theatrical illusion. In Calderón's play, Roque's "But wait, ladies and gentlemen" with its insistence on more stories yet to come does the trick. While in

Shakespeare's play, it is Puck who turns the chev'ril glove inside out again:

> If we shadows have offended,
> Think but this, and all is mended;
> That you have but slumb'red here
> While these visions did appear.
> And this weak and idle theme,
> No more yielding but a dream,
> Gentles, do not reprehend . . .
>
> [5.1.425–31]

It is all like a dream, but dreams, illusions, can be very, very real. They can be the foundations societies are built on and they can be more true for the inner self than whatever facade the individual shows the world. In seventeenth-century Spain, "One dreamed," Wardropper says, "of a different world—not necessarily of a better one—in which the forbidden intimate thoughts could be expressed. The daydream had to be saturnalian, orgiastic, of the world-turned-upside-down, of the self-same world of the comedy. An important function of comedy in the Golden Age must be, I suggest, this: to allow a legitimate outlet for illegitimate hopes and thoughts." [Se soñaba en un mundo diferente—no necesariamente mejor—en el que los pensamientos íntimos prohibidos pudieran exteriorizarse. El fantaseo tenía que ser saturnal, orgiástico, de "mundo al revés," del mismísimo mundo de la comedia. Una importante función de la comedia del Siglo de Oro sería—sugiero—ésta: proporcionar una salida legítima a pensamientos y aspiraciones ilegítimos.][18]

Comedy and the carnivalesque are, unquestionably, escape valves for the tensions and frustrations of the period, but though they permit a glimpse of another world, they do not resolve any of the real problems of this one, nor should we ask them to. They are emblematic of the desire for change and of the real resistance to it. In these plays, characters rush about searching for some authority on which to ground their beliefs, yet they cannot believe what they hear or see. What authority they do find turns out to be, more often than not, either a tautology which communicates little or nothing in its self-referentiality, or a hoary, entrenched figure whose arbitrariness more often licenses speculation than answers it. The characters, then, are caught up in receding layers of illusion that the audience can laugh at, but only ambiguously, for if they look carefully, they will see themselves, their masks, their hopes, fears, and dreams.

## Notes

1. C. L. Barber, *Shakespeare's Festive Comedy* (Princeton: Princeton University Press, 1972), p. 5.
2. José del Corral, *El Madrid de los Austrias* (Madrid: Editorial Avapiés, 1987), pp. 103–4. All translations from Spanish to English are mine. The Spanish text follows:

> En enero, Circuncisión y Reyes; en febrero, Purificación y San Matías; in marzo, San José y la Anunciación; en mayo, San Felipe, Santiago el Menorconocido en Madrid por Santiago el Verde . . . las fiestas fueron aumentando a lo largo de la centuria con el nacimiento de nuevos miembros de la Real Familia, cuyos natalicios y santos se celebraban, así como bautizos, bodas . . . [tanto como se celebraban] entradas y salidas de la Corte.

3. Bruce W. Wardropper, *La comedia española del Siglo de Oro* published with *Teoría de la comedia* by Elder Olson (Barcelona: Editorial Ariel, 1978), p. 209. Spanish text:

> Las fiestas (el Carnaval, en particular) son la institución por medio del cual la sociedad otorga su sanción al comportamiento antisocial bajo condiciones preestablecidas y sólo transitorias. . . . La comedia, expresión teatral de esa energía psíquica antisocial, tiene su origen en las reuniones festivas y los usos galantes de los jóvenes.

4. Mikhail Bakhtin, *Rabelais and His World*, trans. Helene Iswolsky (Bloomington: Indiana University Press, 1984), pp. 196–277.
5. Terry Eagleton, *William Shakespeare* (Oxford: Blackwell, 1986), p. 1.
6. Wardropper, *La comedia*, pp. 217–21.
7. Tirso de Molina, *El vergonzoso en palacio*, ed. Francisco Ayala (Madrid: Editorial Castalia, 1971).
8. Wardropper, *La comedia*, p. 216.
9. J. H. Elliott, *The Count-Duke of Olivares* (New Haven: Yale University Press, 1986), p. 171.
10. Eagleton, *William Shakespeare*, p. 13.
11. Pedro Calderón de la Barca, *Mañana será otro día*, in *Obras completas, tomo 2*, ed. A. Valbuena Briones (Madrid: Aguilar, 1960), pp. 755–99. All quotations are from this edition; all translations mine.
12. Don Esplandián, extraordinary son of the original Spanish chivalric hero, Amadís of Gaul. The son's adventures are recounted in *Las sergas de Esplandián*.
13. Malcolm Evans, "Deconstructing Shakespeare's Comedies," in *Alternative Shakespeares*, ed. John Drakakis (London: Methuen, 1985), p. 74.
14. Terry Eagleton's deflating phrase in his *Literary Theory* (Minneapolis: University of Minnesota Press, 1983), p. 146.
15. Ibid., p. 91.
16. Arnold Reichenberger, "The Uniqueness of the *Comedia*," *Hispanic Review* 27 (1959): 303–16.
17. Eagleton, *William Shakespeare*, p. 22.
18. Wardropper, *La Comedia*, p. 232.

# "But Not for Love": Lope's *El ganso de oro* and *As You Like It*

Frederick A. de Armas
*The Pennsylvania State University*

DURING the last decades of the sixteenth century, Lope de Vega and Shakespeare were concerned with the presentation of pastoral upon the stage. According to Richard Glenn, "Lope's dramatic formula in his early plays is in essence the synthesizing of many elements which he borrowed from different interpretations of the pastoral convention: the Spanish pastoral drama as conceived by Encina and his imitators, and the Spanish pastoral romances."[1] *Comedias* such as *El verdadero amante* and *Belardo furioso*, through the intrusion of autobiographical elements, introduce antipastoral themes such as *interés*. But it is *El ganso de oro* (1588–95)[2] that most clearly exemplifies the move away from the pastoral and toward the historical drama. *As You Like It* (1599) parallels this *comedia* in Shakespeare's production. According to Thomas McFarland, the English play tests the limits of the pastoral convention through the assault of bitterness and alienation upon the bucolic vision, triggering an action that "glances off the dark borders of tragedy."[3] After this, Shakespeare forgoes the pastoral and finds the idea of a joyous society a difficult one to dramatize until his late plays, where the pastoral theme resurfaces in *The Tempest*.[4] David Young proposes a similar movement but shows how the romance plot pattern of characters cast off from society under circumstances that necessitate a pastoral sojourn, although "playfully subverted" in *As You Like It*, is "put to the service of unpleasant fact" in *King Lear* before triumphing in *The Winter's Tale* and *The Tempest*.[5] Although we can hardly deny the move away from the combination of comedy and pastoral after *As You Like It*, most critics would not agree with the foregrounding of tragic or bitter elements in the play. It is more accurately seen as a "liberating playful fantasy . . . a heaven-sent euphoria," or simply a "blessed relief."[6] This essay will examine the parallels that can be found in these two pivotal plays from Spain and England, taking as a point of departure a curiously similar passage in *El ganso de oro* and *As You Like It* where mock rhetoric brings into question the harmonious and nurturing nature of pastoral and the language of romance.[7]

The action of *As You Like It* moves from the court to the countryside, the forest of Arden, where Rosalind, disguised as Ganymede, listens to Orlando's laments on her supposed absence in a scene during the fourth act, which, according to Bertrand Evans, constitutes the climactic peak of the play. Its function, he explains, is to exploit the gap between the awareness of the two lovers.[8] Patrick Swinden claims that as a "corrective against the inflated and vulnerable romantic verse"[9] of Orlando, Rosalind adopts an alternate verbal strategy when she states:

> The poor world is almost six thousand years old, and in all this time there was not any man died in his own person, videlicet, in a love cause. Troilus had his brains dashed out with a Grecian club, yet he did what he could to die before, and he is one of the patterns of love. Leander, he would have lived many a fair year though Hero had turned nun, if it had not been for a hot mid summer night; for, good youth, he went but forth to wash him in the Hellespont, and being taken with the cramp, was drowned, and the foolish chroniclers of that age found it was Hero of Sestos. But these are all lies: men have died from time to time and worms have eaten them, but not for love.[10]

This "diatribe against the doctrine of the broken heart has become a classic," asserts Mark Van Doren, and many critics have chosen to focus on this passage in their analysis of *As You Like It*. For William Scott, Rosalind behaves here as a distant Petrarchan lady who belittles her lover's woes. But passage and scene not only represent the polarity and gap between the two lovers, they also show Rosalind as someone who can reconcile opposites within the self. Her brilliance, according to Jack Vaughn, consists in her being at once "passionate, changeable, mocking, loving." For Peter Phialas, it is the reconciliation of judgment and feeling that characterizes her. Indeed, Rosalind takes it upon herself to examine and criticize, traits which according to Young are characteristic of the pastoral. Her generalizations, he adds, tend to stress her doubts about the success of love. Hers is a paradoxical response to the holiday world, a "smiling sadness," in the words of A. P. Riemer. Or, as C. L. Barber explains, her words express "not sorrow that men die from time to time, but that they do not die for love, that love is not so final as romance would have it."[11]

Rosalind, in these few words, subverts and evokes, denies and desires the world of myth and romance that takes shape in the pastoral retreat. The authority conferred upon these masterful lines by later critics has served to highlight the importance of the passage. However, few delve into contextual or intertextual questions. In his pioneering work on mythology in Shakespeare, Douglas Bush shows how there is a marked change in the use of classical allusions in the mature comedies: "Vestiges of serious Ovidian rhetoric are few . . . The great bulk of allusions in these plays are comic and are in prose. . . . Rosalind, for instance, debunks the notion that Troilus and Leander died of love."[12] Richard Knowles, in what is perhaps the most thorough study of classical myth in *As You Like It*, focuses on the figure of Hercules and consequently disregards this passage.[13] J. J. M. Tobin does point to a clear antecedent, providing further proof that the debunking of the Hero and Leander tale may derive from Thomas Nashe's *Lenten Stuffe* (1599).[14] But, Hallett Smith develops a more convincing argument. Noting that in Shakespeare's main source, Thomas Lodge's *Rosalynde* (1590), there is a reference to the constant Troilus and the loving Leander, this critic proposes that a debunking of the Daphne myth in the romance led Shakespeare through *contaminatio* to transform the references to Troilus and Leander into comic ones.[15] Smith admits that the problem may be more complicated since the reference to Leander may be related to Christopher Marlowe's poem *Hero and Leander*, published in 1598. After all, Phebe had already quoted a line from the poem in the previous act, and there are other allusions to Marlowe in the play that have puzzled scholars for many years.[16]

These discoveries add richness to the passage through contextual reenforcement without altering its authority and originality. However, comparison with certain lines from *El ganso de oro* may provide a new and more problematic context, but one that may lead to a deeper understanding of the uniqueness of these two compositions. In the first act of the *comedia,* the shepherd Pradelo is as prolific and excessive in his love rhetoric as Orlando in *As You Like It*. Both pairs of lovers are situated in a pastoral environment that serves to highlight their amorous concerns. In his desire to impress Lisena, Pradelo threatens to commit suicide and alludes to the myth of Iphis and Anaxerete:

> I am going to hang myself from a tree, just to see if Heaven will turn Lisena and her heart of ice into marble.
>
>> Voy a colgarme de un árbol
>> sólo para ver si el cielo
>> convierte a Lisena en mármol
>> ese corazón de hielo.[17]

Lisena's reaction to Pradelo's threat parallels Rosalind's view of Orlando's statement: "Then in mine own person, I die" (4.1.88). Both women view the threat of suicide by their lovers with skepticism, claiming that few have died for love. Lisena's reply exhibits striking similarities with Rosalind's lines:

> You men are such that you are always deceiving us pretending that you kill yourselves, but very little blood is spilled from the many that so die. If Leander perished, it was because he could go no further, for he certainly did try to leave behind the water that he was forced to drink. Pyramus, as is well-known, fell on his own sword as he tripped on a branch and Iphis, on climbing, was caught on the bars of his beloved's window. To think that anyone has died for love is a lie.

> Sois los hombres desta suerte,
> que siempre nos engañáis
> con fingirnos que os dais muerte,
> y de cuantos os matáis
> muy poca sangre se vierte.
> Que si Leandro murió,
> fue porque no pudo más,
> que no poco porfió
> por dejar el agua atrás
> que tan por fuerza bebió.
> Píramo, como es su fama,
> sobre el espada cayó,
> tropezando en una rama,
> y Isis subiendo se asió
> de una reja de su dama.
> Que pensar que por amor
> ha muerto nadie, es mentira.
> 
> [P. 155]

Both speeches respond to the suicide threat through a generalizing statement that questions the historical existence of male deaths in a love cause. The passages then proceed to specific examples taken from classical mythology in order to deauthorize them. Shakespeare's Rosalind gives two examples, while Lope's Lisena provides three. Finally, there is a conclusion which stresses the mendacity of such legendary tales. "But these are all lies," asserts Rosalind, while Lisena simply states, "es mentira."

Lisena's first example coincides with Rosalind's last. By telling her would-be lover that Leander did not commit suicide but that his drowning was accidental, Lisena is falsifying the ancient myth since in the original Leander's death was never ascribed to suicide. It was Hero, Leander's beloved, who on discovering his body washed ashore jumped from her tower and did die for love. Lisena's falsification is particularly serious: this was a well-known myth and one that enjoyed a special fame, having been recorded by Musaeus, a poet thought to be as ancient as Orpheus.[18] For the Renaissance and the sixteenth century, earlier means closer to the archetypal truth, so that Lisena is here subverting a quasi-sacred text. Interestingly, this myth, according to Marcia Welles, enjoyed less of a vogue in Medieval Spain than in other European countries since it was too openly sensual. With Juan Boscán's adaptation it acquired a new sense of respectability since this poet changed Hero's personality and eliminated problematic scenes. Luis de Góngora parodied the story in "Arrojose el mancebito" (1589) and later in "Aunque entiendo poco griego" (1610).[19] This might be one of the contexts in which Lisena's speech could be studied. After all, the play is entitled *El ganso de oro* and Lope was often equated with the goose due to his natural style while Góngora's *culteranismo* endowed him with the title of swan.[20] If Lope accepts the low language of the goose, he points to its golden nature, the transmuting power of poetry. On the other hand, he has a rustic indulge in the type of parody that Góngora was composing.

Rosalind's transgression is somewhat different, but there is a sense of *ampilificatio* in it. It is as if Shakespeare had taken note of Lope de Vega's text and wished to compound Lisena's lies, her subversion of an authoritative text. Rosalind rewrites the myth making an even more extravagant claim: Leander did not die while swimming to meet Hero. The use of language is particularly effective here in bringing down the loftiness of the original and possibly the tone of a contemporary version, Marlowe's *Hero and Leander*. Rosalind states that Hero "had turned nun," an anachronistic and mocking way to refer to her role as priestess of Aphrodite. This could well be a reminiscence of Marlowe's "Venus' Nun,"[21] although deprived of its antithetical nature. Furthermore, Rosalind tells Orlando that Hero's position did not worry Leander, who would have lived a long life had he not wished to bathe in the Hellespont. Leander's death, then, has little to do with heroic or amorous pursuits. He was not attempting to reach his beloved nor was he in the midst of a dangerous undertaking. He was indifferent to Hero. His status is further deflated by the manner of his death: he "was taken with the cramp" and died. Significantly, not a word is said here either of Hero's suicide. On the contrary, Musaeus and other ancient authorities that point to Hero as the cause of Leander's death are called "foolish chroniclers." The audience may wonder if such a name should also be applied to Marlowe.

While Lope de Vega stresses the accidental nature of deaths attributed to amorous passion, Shakespeare adds the indifference of the lover. In Rosalind's re-creation of the myth, Leander seems to care little for Hero, while in Lisena's description he drowns as he swims to reach her. Lisena's two other examples also follow the pattern of accidental deaths, which diminish their romantic and tragic significance. Pyramus trips on a branch and falls upon his sword, while Iphis gets caught as he climbs to see Anaxerete. Lisena concludes with this example since it had been used by Pradelo to formulate his suicide threat. This third myth is different from the other two in that the woman in the original tale does not reciprocate the man's love. In this sense, it comes closer to the actual situation between Lisena and Pradelo. This lack of mutuality in love links Lisena's third example to Rosalind's first. The tale of Troilus and Cressida in Benoit de Sainte-Maure, Boccaccio, and Chaucer, depicts an innocent young warrior betrayed by the fickle Cressida, who finds a new lover in the enemy's camp during the Trojan war. Rosalind cleverly shifts the focus of the tale. She does not blame the woman, but points to Troilus. By Shakespeare's time, he had become a character most amenable to debunking as Ann Thompson informs us. The reputation of his beloved Cressida and of her uncle Pandarus had much declined in Elizabethan times and, "given such company, even Troilus cannot remain uncontaminated, but is the subject of ridicule, as in Petruchio's use of the name for his spaniel *(Taming of the Shrew*, 4.1.134) and in Rosalind's jocular reference."[22] Troilus' heroic death is deflated through language, "his brains dashed out with a Grecian club." But here Rosalind is closer to the truth of legend since Troilus' death had more to do with the Trojan war than with Cressida. Studying Shakespeare's play on the subject, David Jago explains: "The point of *Troilus and Cressida* is not that men are dominated by corrupt love, but that sexual emotion is cast aside by men in their roles as social beings as soon as it threatens to hinder society's main preoccupation: honor, either personal or national."[23] Through these examples, Lisena and Rosalind present two patterns of love, mutual and one-sided. They attempt to show that truth is much less inspiring and more mundane than legend, pointing to accidents and indifference on the part of the male suitors. Although the unrequited lovers Troilus and Iphis receive less chastisement than Leander in the speeches of the two shepherdesses, language and situation still debunk their myths. Only the tale of Pyramus, which occupies the central position in Lisena's examples, does not seem to have a counterpart in Rosalind's speech. And yet, it will be argued that traces of it can be found elsewhere in *As You Like It,* thus completing and commenting on Lope's *El ganso de oro.*

These parallels may point to a tradition from which both Lope and Shakespeare drew this diatribe against the broken heart or they may reflect a synchronic development of these two national theaters. The similarities in setting, situation, and characterization should also lead to the investigation of the possibility of direct influence.[24] The intertextual connections serve to enrich both texts and show the parallel, yet unique, approach taken by each playwright in the presentation of pastoral, myth, and romance.

In *El ganso de oro* the pastoral ambience is restricted to the first act and occasional scenes afterwards. The action here "derives mainly from the traditional motif of the chain of lovers. Three shepherds and two shepherdesses, Belardo, Silvero, Pradelo, Lisena, and Belisa, are hopelessly in love with the wrong man or woman."[25] Only one couple, Belardo-Belisa, show reciprocity.[26] All assiduously seek these positive and negative love experiences since they serve to generate the one type of speech that is relished in Arcadia—a rhetoric of love that ranges from the lament for unrequited passion to the seductive language that attempts to bind the love object to oneself. The artificiality of the ambience is made evident by Lisena, who repeatedly punctures the poetic world that her would-be lover seeks to construct. In answer to Pradelo's seductive rhetoric, she exclaims: "You have made me into a garden" (Toda me has hecho un jardín, p. 154), thus reducing his botanical conceits to laughter. It is when Pradelo's strategy turns from seduction to lament, alluding to the myth of Iphis, that Lisena debunks the notion of dying for love.

Shakespeare's play begins at the treacherous court of the usurping duke. A "golden world," equated with the forest of Arden, is thus sought by many. It is to this place that the old Duke and his followers have retired, an oasis described by Renato Poggioli as belonging to certain pastoral patterns, and a sojourn considered by Young as typical of Shakespeare's plays that follow the pastoral romance form.[27] The third and fourth acts show the audience that this locale is not only the peaceful refuge of those that flee the corruption of the court, an oasis that recalls the tranquility of the mythical golden world, the first age of humankind, but that this example of the *beatus ille* motif is also a pastoral milieu where the tangled loves of shepherds and shepherdesses and those disguised as such can be enacted. Phebe and Silvius in *As You Like It* parallel Lisena and Pradelo in *El ganso de oro* as rustics whose language is above their station in life. This is "the essential trick of the old pastoral," according to William Empson, "to make simple people express strong feelings (felt as the most universal subject, something fundamentally true about everybody) in learned and fashionable language."[28] But this essential pastoral notion is brought into question by both Lisarda and Phebe. We have seen how Lisena has laughed at Pradelo's botanical conceits and at his threat of suicide. Phebe also criticizes Silvius, for example when he claims that her eyes can wound and even kill him (3.5.28–31).

Neither pair, Lisena-Pradelo, Phebe-Silvius, seem inclined to show reciprocity in love. Lisena's disdain for Pradelo mirrors the mythical Anaxerete's coldness toward Iphis. Lisena's mutability, on the other hand, is akin to that of Cressida. Phebe is also an Anaxerete figure. She turns her back on Silvius and falls for Ganymede, who is none other than the disguised Rosalind. Phebe-Silvius are considered "a fine example of the subtle effects Shakespeare derives from his middle level mirror image characters."[29] Although she mocks Silvius in a manner similar to Rosalind's criticism toward Orlando, she is not interested in the shepherd, but aims her love higher at Rosalind-Ganymede. Lisena acts in a similar fashion and desires Belardo over Pradelo. Both shepherdesses neglect their equals and in their desire point to the idealized noble couples, Orlando-Rosalind and Belardo-Belisa. Pastoral characters played by the nobility are thus portrayed as superior and more desirable than the actual inhabitants of the forest of Arden or of Arcadia. This brings into question the nature of the golden world in these dramas.

In a recent article, A. Stuart Daley, noting images of cold, hunger, hunting, sickness, wounds, and pursuit in *As You Like It*, concludes that: "All the major dramatic elements agree in denying moral superiority to the countryside."[30] Although such a statement represents a critical extreme that must be tempered by the realization of the benefic influence of the forest on the exiles, it does alert us to a questioning of the pastoral in *As You Like It*. A similar situation is found in *El ganso de oro*. Here, the idyllic land is disturbed by the presence of a *salvaje* who delights in abducting beautiful maidens. His savage chase recalls the image of the wounded stag in Shakespeare's play:

> The wretched animal heav'd forth such groans
> That their discharge did stretch his leathern coat

> Almost to bursting, and the big round tears
> Coursed one another down his innocent nose
> In piteous chase. . . .
>
> [P. 32]

Such a scene would be inconceivable in a true golden world where nature gives bountifully to humankind without the need for hunting or even agriculture.[31] Thus, the forest of Arden is not as Charles imagined, akin to the mythical golden age, but is a typical pastoral setting where death and violence coexist with quiet recollection. Both the savage and the hunted stag can also point to the passions that are unfolded in this land. The image of man as hunter and of woman as his prey is a common one in the period, and so is the intrusion of the lustful savage upon an idyllic setting, as for example in Jorge de Montemayor's *La Diana*.[32] Both Arcadia and the forest of Arden house human beings that exhibit humoral imbalances, from the melancholy Jaques to the amorous Orlando, and from the melancholy Belisa to the choleric Silvero. Pastoral becomes a landscape of the spirit, according to David Young, "recording mental events and psychological states."[33] But in *El ganso de oro* these characters lack a life of their own and are caught in the myth of Arcadia.

In *El ganso de oro* Lisena does not emerge as a strong character since her rebellion against the language that imprisons her in the Arcadian way of life is short lived. When she sees Belardo poeticizing his love for Belisa through an apostrophe to nature (p. 156), she no longer seeks to puncture the language of love, but in her jealousy turns it against herself, using the very image of suicide that she had once rejected: "that I am going to hang myself from a noose formed from the oldest and strongest vine" (que voy a ahorcarme en los lazos / de la vid mas firme y vieja, p. 158). Lisena soon forgets Belardo for Silvero, a shepherd with whom she pretended to be in love in order to arouse the passion and jealousy of Belardo. Both Pradelo and Silvero, Lisena's rustic would-be lovers, are named after the environment in which they live. The first name recalls a *prado* while the second derives from a sylvan locale. In this sense, they parallel Phebe's Silvius, a name that does not stem from Shakespeare's main source, Thomas Lodge's *Rosalynd*, but could be another indication of *El ganso de oro*'s possible influence on the English comedy.

The main couple in *El ganso de oro* does not rebel but actually revels in the language of Arcadia. Belisa does not mirror Lisena since she delights in Belardo's love rhetoric, which ranges from apostrophes to nature (pp. 156–57) to the discussion of the representation of the beloved's name on a *tablilla* through the use of two letters, *b* and *a,* and a picture of a flower, the *lis* (p. 158). Lacking strong characterization with which to hold the audience's attention, the *comedia* soon abandons the countryside. The play's first act presents and destroys the illusion of Arcadia as a land where the myth of the golden age is actualized. It is a static land where love is expressed through a rhetoric whose artificiality undermines real feeling or where loss and lament lead to thoughts of suicide. Arcadia is a place that is in the process of destroying itself. The dream serves only to point toward desired harmony and the struggle must take place in the social world.

*As You Like It* does not share this movement, since it begins at the court, providing the motivation for the journey to the forest. It is as if the historical world is too corrupt to alllow the emergence of a comic vision that yearns for the golden world. Pastoral, in Shakespeare's vision, is a half-way land between myth and history. It can incorporate the melancholy Jaques and the foolish Touchstone, rustics and feigned shepherds. For in the forest of Arden there is winter and death, but there is also time to explore the self and the passions in an environment that nourishes those that seek refuge. It approaches a maternal landscape,[34] maintaining, revivifying, and secure. It may also be a literary and stylized space, but is one where human interaction is easy, where differences are easily tolerated and transcended. It thus comes close to representing the *coincidentia oppositorum* of the alchemists and Neoplatonists. Joseph Westlund describes the ease of Arden thus: "we get a glimpse of part of our life which we usually pay little attention to: times when we feel at ease with a variety of feelings which are not felt with much intensity of conflict, and when kind and generous responses make us feel part of a benign world."[35] Even the responses of Rosalind-Ganymede to Orlando fail to create a discordant tension, for the audience knows her love for him. The mock rhetoric is a playful manner of teaching and testing her beloved as well as probing the limits of love. Nothing could be further from the stereotyped Belisa than the brilliant Rosalind. She does not belong to the corrupt world of Duke Frederick nor does she accept myth uncritically. Perhaps Barber is correct in detecting a note of sorrow in her realization that "love is not so final as romance would have it."[36] But paradoxically Rosalind finds mythical fulfillment through the example omitted by her but central to Lisena's speech against the suicidal lovers.

If Orlando does not prove his love for Rosalind in death, he does evince the capacity to love herocially when he encounters his brother Oliver threatened by a lioness. He thinks of leaving him to his fate since Oliver had been responsible for Orlando's exile and had even attempted to kill him. But fraternal love triumphs. Orlando battles the lioness to save his brother. He then sends a bloodied napkin to Rosalind in order to prove to her that his wound had prevented him from being on time for their meeting. The lioness and a cloth besmeared with blood are key elements to the tragic story of Pyramus and Thisbe, the central example used by Lisena on the doctrine of the broken heart. On seeing the bloodied veil dripped by Thisbe and smeared with blood by the lioness, Pyramus, sure of her death, commits suicide (although in Lisena's version he accidentally falls on his sword). In *As You Like It*, Rosalind's omission of this myth in her examples is coupled with the discovery of traces of the tale in a scene that demonstrates Orlando's heroic love. If he has risked his life for a brother that would have killed him, what would he not do for Rosalind. The English play thus responds to Lisena's example and Rosalind's doubts by upholding the original myth.

It is only after Orlando has proven himself, adding a mythical dimension to his being, that Rosalind sheds her mocking self and becomes a magician. Magic, then, derives from her positive response to myth. Both of these transformative forces emerge from the depths of the forest of Arden thus revealing the liminality of the region.[37] In *El ganso de oro*, magic erupts as a negative response. Pastoral is seen as a space bound by its rhetoric, as a land that limits possibilities. Felicio, the magician, must point to an exit from Arcadia. The play's last two acts take place for the most part in "historical" time. It is here—and not in a pastoral setting—that Belardo can exhibit his nature as a mythical hero. He slays the dragon and thus frees the city of Naples from contagion. The shepherd Belardo is proclaimed king of Naples since he is the hero that has brought health to the land. Other inhabitants of Arcadia must now emerge from their sheltered realm and act out their passions and desires to bring about a resolution. Felicio orchestrates events so as to balance perspectives and reconcile opposites. The magician's name underlines the happiness that he will bring about. His powers are akin to those of the playwright who can bring together disparate elements into a cohesive and artistic whole. Relying on the anagnorisis of romance, Belardo and Belisa are discovered to be children of kings. The jealous Silvero, who lifts an invisible dagger to murder Belardo, is shown to be his brother. An imminent fratricide is transformed into a joyous reconciliation.

The rivalry among brothers had also been central to the tension in *As You Like it:* Duke Senior had been deposed by his younger brother; Orlando had almost been killed by Oliver. The English play thus reveals a similar mythical opposition as the *comedia*. But Shakespeare shows that magic is to be found *within* the pastoral oasis: the young duke wishes to attack his brother but is converted as he attempts to penetrate the magical circle of Arden. It is in the tranquil spaces of the forest that the truth of human potential is revealed, leading to a fleeting glimpse of the golden world. While Shakespeare recalls the mythical age through the contemplation and self-examination of a pastoral oasis, Lope de Vega shows Arcadia to be a false paradise and moves toward the actualization of a golden age in history through the actions of Belardo, although it is Felicio, the playwright as magus, who allows us this vision. In *As You Like It,* magic is first manifested in Rosalind's loving response to Orlando's self-revelation. She comes to believe in the very myths she subverts, while preserving a playful attitude toward love. She revels in love's finality but deprives it of its tragic strains. Margaret Boerner Beckman claims that "to know Rosalind is to know that opposites can be reconciled."[38] And indeed *discordia concors* is a basic tenet of the Renaissance magus. The assumption of this new role by Rosalind is reflected in her language. We move from mock rhetoric to what Karen Newman describes as a "language which hints, in its formal balance and repetition, at a magician's spell." Rosalind's enchanting impulse seems to saturate the play: "It is almost as if the characters are under a spell or a trance."[39]

It is at this point that the power and nature of the forest is fully revealed. As a liminal space, it brings forth all possibilities. On the one hand, the mythical is fully lively through the appearance of the god Hymen, who will preside over the weddings. This has been called one of the most magical moments of the play: "*As You Like It* invites us to conceive of the difficult magic of two opposites existing simultaneously, truly contrary and mutually exclusive, but bound together in a creative if paradoxical union—like man and wife."[40] On the other hand, myth and magic make possible a move toward the historical world. With the conversion of Duke Frederick, all who so wish can return to the court now restored to the old ruler. It is fitting that Rosalind, the magician, utter the epilogue. Her appearance does not dispel the sense of wonder. She exemplifies how the individual can become a veritable magician through the power of *discordia concors*. Her final words also point to the play as a kind of magic which allows everyday reality to become something more, to expand toward happiness and harmony. By representing the playwright as magus, she parallels Felicio's role in the *comedia*.

Both *El ganso de oro* and *As You Like It* are about breaking boundaries. The subversion of myth, the questioning of classical examples, are only strategies that lead the audience to more readily accept the mythification of theatrical space. Both plays are pivotal in their presentation of pastoral, but they move in different directions. Lope de Vega's Arcadia must be abandoned or transformed since it is a limited land, not fit for the possibilities of theater. Shakespeare's forest, on the other hand, transcends dramatic possibilities. While Lope de Vega moves away from Arcadia toward the historical process and proposes action as a way to bring back the first and happiest of ages, Shakespeare sees in the contemplative and liminal spaces[41] of Arden a place where the self can partake of the magic of creation and rekindle the myths of those "foolish chroniclers" that believed in the heroic nature of life and love.

## Notes

1. Richard F. Glenn, "The Impact of the Spanish Pastoral Romance on Lope de Vega's Dramatic Art," *Annali del' Istituto Universitario Orientale* 13 (1971):9.

2. The dating of Lope's play is derived from S. Griswold Morley and Courtney Bruerton, *Cronología de las comedias de Lope de Vega* (Madrid: Gredos, 1968), p. 75.

3. Thomas McFarland, *Shakespeare's Pastoral Comedy* (Chapel Hill: University of North Carolina Press, 1972), p. 101.

4. Ibid., p. 121: "And after *As You Like It*, Shakespeare not only forgoes pastoral therapy for a while, but his comic vessels, leaving behind the clear waters sailed by *Twelfth Night* and *The Merry Wives of Windsor*, begin to labor in heavy seas of bitterness. The idea of the joyous society tends henceforth to be more difficult to achieve and maintain. In *The Winter's Tale*, great cracks run through the artifice of happiness, and are caulked only with great difficulty. Not until *The Tempest* does Shakespeare's art . . . find quiet harbor in a renewed paradisal hope."

5. David Young, *The Heart's Forest: A Study of Shakespeare's Pastoral Art* (New Haven: Yale University Press, 1972), p. 120.

6. Ruth Nevo, *Comic Transformations in Shakespeare* (London: Methuen, 1980), p. 181; Joseph Westlund, *Shakespeare's Reparative Comedies* (Chicago: University of Chicago Press, 1984), p. 75.

7. Few studies have delved into the parallel between Shakespeare and Lope de Vega. An early attempt by Albert R. Frey is useful in that it includes an extensive list of Spanish sources. However, the purpose of the book is to deny or minimize such possibilities. He discusses, for example, Jorge de Montemayor's *La Diana* and *Two Gentlemen of Verona;* Lope's *La hermosura aborrecida* and *All's Well that Ends Well;* the anonymous play *La española en Florencia* and *Twelfth Night;* Lope's *El caballero de Olmedo* and *The Taming of the Shrew;* Lope's *El mármol de Felisardo* and *The Winter's Tale;* Lope's *Castelvines y Monteses* and *Romeo*

*and Juliet;* Lope's *Las flores de Don Juan* and *As You Like It.* In *William Shakespeare and Alleged Spanish Prototypes* (New York: Shakespeare Society, 1886). Henry Thomas, in *Shakespeare and Spain* (Oxford: Clarendon Press, 1922), presents a more balanced conclusion: "The *Two Gentlemen of Verona* owes something to Montemayor's *Diana* and *The Winter's Tale* to *Amadis de Grecia. The Tempest* is at any rate related to Eslava's *Noches de Invierno,* even if Shakespeare knew nothing of the Spanish book. His apparent allusion to *The Mirror of Knighthood* may warrant the suspicion that he read, and perhaps utilized, that romance; and we at least speculate as to whether he came under the influence of Cervantes and the *Celestina*" (p. 31). For other early studies see Selma Gutlman, *The Foreign Sources of Shakespeare's Works* (New York: King's Crown Press, 1947). There have been several recent studies on the subject: Walter Cohen, for example, compares *As You Like It* with Lope's *Los donaires de Matico* in *Drama of a Nation* (Ithaca: Cornell University Press, 1985), pp. 193–94; Donald R. Hadley in "Lope and Shakespeare," *The American Hispanist* 4 (January-February 1979): 13–19, discusses the parallels between Lope's *Castelvines y Monteses* and Shakespeare's *Romeo and Juliet,* also pointing to a three-act manuscript play, *Otelo, o sea el moro de Venecia,* which was written almost at the same time as Shakespeare's *Othello* (1603–4). Finally, Laura Leo de Belmont, "Romeo y Julieta en Lope de Vega y Shakespeare," *Revista de Literaturas Modernas* 16 (1983): 147–58 discusses the same plays as Hadley.

8. Bertrand Evans, *Shakespeare's Comedies* (Oxford: Clarendon Press, 1960), pp. 94–95.

9. Patrick Swinden, *An Introduction to Shakespeare's Comedies* (New York: MacMillan, 1973), p. 118.

10. William Shakespeare, *As You Like It,* ed. Agnes Latham, Arden edition (London: Methuen, 1975), 4.1.89–103. All textual references to the play are from this edition.

11. Mark Van Doren, *Shakespeare* (New York: Holt, 1939), p. 158; William Scott, *The God of Arts: Ruling Ideas in Shakespeare's Comedies* (Lawrence: University of Kansas Publications, 1977), pp. 74–75; Jack A. Vaughn, *Shakespeare's Comedies* (New York: Ungar, 1980), pp. 123–24; Peter Phialas, *Shakespeare's Romantic Comedies* (Chapel Hill: University of North Carolina Press, 1966), p. 252; David Young, *The Heart's Forest,* p. 66; A. P. Riemer, *Antic Fables: Patterns of Evasion in Shakespeare's Comedies* (New York: St. Martin's Press, 1980), p. 77; and C. L. Barber, *Shakespeare's Festive Comedy* (Princeton: Princeton University Press, 1959), p. 235.

12. Douglas Bush, "Classical Myth in Shakespeare's Plays," *Elizabethan and Jacobean Studies Presented to Frank Percy Willson,* ed. Herbert Davis and Helen Gardner (Oxford: Clarendon Press, 1959), p. 71.

13. Richard Knowles, "Myth and Type in *As You Like It,*" *English Literary History* 33 (1966): 1–22.

14. J. J. M. Tobin, "New Sources for *As You Like It,*" *English Language Notes* 17 (1980): 172–75.

15. "Daphne, that bony wench, was not turned into a bay tree as the poets feign, but for her chastity her fame was immortal, resembling the laurel that is ever green." In Hallett Smith, *Shakespeare's Romances: A Study of Some Ways of the Imagination* (San Marino, Calif.: The Huntington Library, 1972), pp. 79–80.

16. John Bakeless, *Christopher Marlowe* (New York: William Morrow, 1937), pp. 292–93.

17. Lope de Vega, *El ganso de oro,* ed. Emilio Cotarelo y Mori, *Obras de Lope de Vega,* vol. 1 (Madrid: Real Academia Española, 1916), p. 155. All textual references to the play are to this edition; English translations are mine.

18. Douglas Bush, *Mythology and the Renaissance Tradition in English Poetry* (Minneapolis: University of Minnesota Press, 1932), pp. 139–55.

19. Marcia L. Welles, *Arachne's Tapestry: The Transformation of Myth in Seventeenth-Century Spain* (San Antonio, Texas: Trinity University Press, 1986), pp. 19–37; see also Erich Segal, "Hero and Leander: Góngora and Marlowe," *Comparative Literature* 15 (1963): 338–56.

20. On the swan-goose opposition see Marcia L. Welles, *Arachne's Tapestry,* p. 47. In

Vergil's ninth eclogue the goose is the bad poet who cackles among tuneful swans. See Fernando Lázaro Carreter, "Situación de la Fábula de Píramo y Tisbe," *Nueva Revista de Filología Hispánica* 15 (1961): 481. The rivalry between Góngora and Lope was already apparent in the 1580s and 1590s. See Emilio Orozco Díaz, *Lope y Góngora frente a frente* (Madrid: Gredos, 1973).

21. T. W. Baldwin, *Shakespeare's Five-Act Structure* (Urbana: University of Illinois Press, 1947), p. 645.

22. Ann Thompson, *Shakespeare's Chaucer* (New York: Barnes and Noble, 1978), p. 65. This passage is not discussed in E. Talbot Donaldson, *The Swan at the Well: Shakespeare Reading Chaucer* (New Haven: Yale University Press, 1985).

23. David M. Jago, "The Uniqueness of *Troilus and Cressida*," *Shakespeare Quarterly* 29 (1978): 22.

24. *El ganso de oro* was edited in 1916 by Emilio Cotarelo y Mori from a manuscript copy. Even if an early edition were to exist, it would be unlikely that Shakespeare would have known it.

25. Glenn, "The Impact of the Spanish Pastoral Romance," p. 16.

26. Belardo and Belisa are the names that Lope de Vega used to incorporate himself and his beloved Isabel de Urbina in his texts. For a detailed treatment of Lope's use of autobiographical material see Alan S. Trueblood, *Experience and Artistic Expression in Lope de Vega: The Making of "La Dorotea"* (Cambridge: Harvard University Press, 1974).

27. Renato Poggioli, "The Oaten Flute," *Harvard Library Bulletin* 11 (1957): 147–84; Young, *The Heart's Forest*, p. 20.

28. William Empson, *Some Versions of Pastoral* (Norfolk, Conn.: New Directions, 1935), p. 11.

29. Ruth Nevo, *Comic Transformations in Shakespeare*, p. 199; Richard Levin, *The Multiple Plot in English Renaissance Drama* (Chicago: University of Chicago Press, 1971).

30. A. Stuart Daley, "Dispraise of the Country in *As You Like It*," *Shakespeare Quarterly* 36 (1985): 300–314.

31. Harry Levin, *The Myth of the Golden Age in the Renaissance* (Oxford: Oxford University Press, 1969). *As You Like It* is discussed on pp. 122–23.

32. Edith Randam Rodgers, *The Perilous Hunt: Symbols in Hispanic and European Balladry* (Lexington: University Press of Kentucky, 1980).

33. Young, *The Heart's Forest*, p. 31.

34. Richard Wheeler, *Shakespeare's Development and the Problem Comedies: Turn and Counter-Turn* (Berkeley: University of California Press, 1981), p. 175.

35. Westlund, *Shakespeare's Reparative Comedies*, p. 75.

36. Barber, *Shakespeare's Festive Comedy*, p. 121.

37. On liminality as a phenomenon that falls "betwixt and between the positions assigned and arranged by law, custom, convention and ceremonial," see Victor Turner, *The Ritual Process: Structure and Anti-Structure* (Chicago: Aldine, 1969), p. 95.

38. Margaret Boerner Beckman, "The Figure of Rosalind in *As You Like It*," *Shakespeare Quarterly* 29 (1978): 46.

39. Karen Newman, *Shakespeare's Rhetoric of Comic Character* (London: Methuen, 1985), p. 97.

40. Beckman, "The Figure of Rosalind," p. 46.

41. There is a magical cave that separates Arcadia and Naples in *El ganso de oro*. In actuality, of course, the two lands are far apart. It is by entering the cave that Belardo comes in touch with the deeper levels of his self and emerges a hero in the historical world. Thus, the cave is the liminal space between the lands in the *comedia*, in this way resembling the forest of Arden in *As You Like It*. On the significance of caves in Golden Age literature see my study "Caves of Fame and Wisdom in the Spanish Pastoral Novel," *Studies in Philology* 82 (1985): 332–58.

# Tirso's Festive Comedy: *El vergonzoso en palacio* and *As You Like It*

Susan L. Fischer
*Bucknell University*

MARGARET Wilson has observed in passing that Tirso de Molina's *El vergonzoso en palacio* (*The Shy Man at Court* [1621]) "has a surprising number of features in common with *As You Like It*, a play with which it will easily stand comparison."[1] Bruce Wardropper also sees affinities between the two plays, citing C. L. Barber's notion of "festive comedy" to underscore thematic and formal parallels.[2] Barber, in describing the structural pattern of plays of this type, speaks of a "holiday" or "saturnalian" attitude of liberty from normal limitations that "appears in many variations, all of which involve inversion, statement and counterstatement, and a basic movement which can be summarized in the formula, through release to clarification."[3] The first half of *As You Like It*, beginning with tyrant brother and tyrant duke and moving out into the forest of Arden, is chiefly concerned with establishing this sense of festive freedom. Here the traditional contrast of jaded court and transforming sylvan environment is shaped by the contrast between everyday and holiday, or between the normal world and the "green world," where ordinary social standards are reversed and "a many merry men . . . fleet the time carelessly as they did in the golden world."[4] Arden is a place of discovery where individuals find themselves, especially in matters of love. In Arden the love affairs of Orlando and Rosalind, Silvius and Phebe, Touchstone and Audrey, come to flourish; and the betrothal of Oliver and Celia, although scarcely developed, provides the impetus for the movement from the green world back to the normal world. The quadruple wedding festival at the end suggests the potential for both individual integration and social rejuvenation. Tirso's *El vergonzoso en palacio* can be further illuminated by considering it in the context of its Elizabethan counterpart, especially with regard to the seminal issues of love, the pastoral, and the search for individual and social identity.

At first glance, the structural pattern of *El vergonzoso* may appear to be an inversion of that of *As You Like It,* moving from the initial scenes in the forest to the court of Avero, and from a brief interlude in the woodlands back again to the ducal palace. Although the principal setting for the action is not the green wood but the court, the time is that of Carnival (Fiestas de Carnestolendas), a period of revitalizing saturnalian license when ordinary social conventions are temporarily suspended.[5] At the end of the play, the hero's psychosexual transformation and the discovery of his true noble identity cause a new society to crystalize around him which is symbolized, as in Shakespeare, by a quadruple wedding involving Mireno and Magdalena, Antonio and Serafina, Tarso and Melisa, and the Count of Estremoz and Leonela. The pivotal point of comparison between *As You Like It* and *El vergonzoso,* then, lies in the particular nature and function of the love relationship of the hero and heroine in each play, as defined in part by the relationships of the other couples. In Shakespeare as in Tirso, the total point of view is a composite of counterbalancing perspectives which together work to form a properly balanced outlook. The structure of multiple plottings in which numerous groups of characters are thematically played off against one another is achieved by a series of parallels and contrasts, juxtapositions, and variations upon a similar theme. Terry Eagleton observes that there is no "simple antithesis" in *As You Like It,* for binary oppositions are continually modified or "deconstructed,"[6] and the same would apply to *El vergonzoso.*

The opening scenes of both plays reveal the decadent world of the court overrun by its intrigues, vengeances, and traitorous actions. The unnatural circumstances surrounding Mireno's birth and upbringing in the forest of Avero bear comparison to Orlando's life on his brother's estate just outside the "envious court" of Duke Frederick (2.1.4), which has been usurped from its rightful heir, Duke Senior. Orlando's initial complaint is that he is not getting enough education in the pursuit of gentlemanly ways, for he has been kept "rustically at home" (1.1.2–7) by his vicious elder brother Oliver who ironically recognizes the youth's innate nobility: "Yet he's gentle, never schooled and yet learned, full of noble device, of all sorts enchantingly beloved" (1.1.164–66). Nature is not enough for Orlando; he will have nurture too. But he soon learns that one's virtues can be "sanctified and holy traitors" in a world where "what is comely / Envenoms him that bears it" (2.3.12–15). When he defeats Charles the Wrestler, Duke Frederick, discovering his parentage, arbitrarily casts him aside, saying: "The world esteem'd thy father honourable / But I did find him still mine enemy" (1.2.214–15). Thus the "envious court" is a place where brothers turn unnaturally against brothers: the younger Frederick wrongfully seizes Duke Senior's throne, and the elder Oliver denies the younger Orlando his birthright of education. In still another parallel, Orlando and Rosalind are held guilty by association, mistrusted as the son and daughter of Frederick's political enemies, Sir Rowland de Boys and Duke Senior. "Thou art thy father's daughter, there's enough" (1.3.54), retorts the humorous (or passion-ruled) Frederick in explaining Rosalind's exile from court. Orlando, doubly outcast by brother and duke, is nurtured by the virtuous old Adam, and the two embark on a journey that will take them to the forest of Arden, the refuge of Duke Senior and of his now banished daughter, Rosalind.

Mireno is also the victim of an unnatural upbringing, the result of treasonous actions on the part of his father's political enemies. Almost twenty-one years before the play begins, the Duke of Coimbra, uncle to the young king Alfonso Quinto, had been doubly accused by the treacherous Vasco Fernández, and by the unseasoned heir to the throne, of having poisoned the queen mother. By so having the Duke of Coimbra falsely declared a traitor, Fernández, now a sycophantic counselor, gains power over a king not old enough to rule and throws the kingdom into disorder. The banished Duke of Coimbra now lives in the forest disguised as the shepherd Lauro, and his son Mireno, born in exile, is as yet ignorant of the circumstances surrounding his birth. Nonetheless Mireno is conscious at some level of an innate nobility that is his by rights. He is troubled by thoughts and impulses generated by his "inflated imagination" (altiva imaginación)[7] which he does not understand. The following words addressed to his companion Tarso (a *gracioso* or fool figure) reveal a frustrated drive toward self-actualization that parallels Orlando's strong desire not to be kept "rustically at home," but to be nurtured in accordance with his noble nature:

> Considero algunos ratos
> que los cielos, que pudieron
> hacerme noble, y me hicieron
> un pastor, fueron ingratos;
> y que, pues con tal bajeza
> me acobardo y avergüenzo,
> puedo poco, pues no venzo
> mi misma naturaleza.
>
> [1.351–58]

> I've thought about this, and I know
> the heavens could have made of me
> a nobleman, and yet you see
> me shepherd; what a cruel blow.
> And this low station strikes me dumb;
> I am timid and filled with shame;
> I can do little, and the blame's
> the nature I can't overcome.

Mireno's daring imagination even causes him to doubt his father's humble demeanor and speech because a nobler essence shines forth from within:

> . . . su mucha discreción
> dice claro que es postizo
> su grosero oficio y traje.
>
> [1.377–79]
>
> . . . his good judgment shows
> his lowly manners and his dress
> are nothing more than a disguise.

Ultimately he is moved by these lofty thoughts to seek his fortune elsewhere:

> . . . que a buscar me desmande
> lo que mi estrella destina,
> que a cosas grandes me inclina
> y algún bien me aguarda grande.
>
> [1.395–98]
>
> What my stars hold, my destiny,
> I'm thus impelled to go and find:
> for to great deeds I am inclined
> and some great fortune waits for me.

The elements of evil which have condemned Mireno to exile from birth, and which in parallel fashion have undermined the advantages of gentility due Orlando by virtue of his heritage, are brought to the fore in scenes which precede and follow Mireno's initial appearance. The jealous and usurping forces obstructing both the kingdom of Portugal and the dukedom of Avero surface early on in a confrontation between the Duke of Avero and the Count of Estremoz during a hunt in which the former is wrongly accused of having signed a letter condemning the latter to death. Although the Duke convinces the Count of his innocence, the Duke's startled reaction—"Am I in my right mind or mad?"

(¿Estoy despierto o loco?, 1.44)—reflects the atmosphere of dissimulation and disorder that pervades his world.[8] The Duke soon learns that the author of the perfidious letter is his former secretary Ruy Lorenzo, but what he does not know is that the Count is hardly the innocent victim he seems, for he has dishonored Leonela, sister of Ruy Lorenzo, who then forged the signature in order to effect his revenge. Thus the Count's first words to the Duke—"No more pretenses" (Basta el disimular, 1.9)—are laden with irony and heighten the duplicity of the courtly scene.

In another part of the forest, Ruy Lorenzo and his servant Vasco are seeking to escape justice and happen upon Mireno who, upon hearing their tale of woe, offers a shepherd's disguise in exchange for "noble attire" (las galas del traje noble, 1.605). The search for identity in festive comedy, according to Frye, entails a phase of temporarily lost identity, confusion, and sexual license, which is often symbolized by the stock device of impenetrable disguise or by the activities of an invisible character like Puck or Ariel.[9] That this search has begun is evidenced at once by Ruy's flight to the forest as the traditional haven for the oppressed, and by Mireno's impending release from a seemingly unencumbered, yet largely restrictive, pastoral existence. Although at present Mireno's disguise represents a period of momentary loss and disorder, it also accentuates his innate nobility and is therefore a potentially natural fit, as Ruy's reaction indicates:

> Pero cuando en ti contemplo
> el desenfado con que andas
> y el donaire con que mandas
> ese vestido, otro ejemplo
> hallo en ti más natural,
> que vuelve por tu decoro,
> llamándote imagen de oro,
> con la funda de sayal.
>
> [1.612–19]

> Yet when I saw the way that you
> walk with such assurance and grace
> and the charming way that you pace
> about in that fine suit, I knew
> your other, more natural side;
> saw your true demeanor unfold.
> You are an image cast in gold
> that your rough sack cloth tries to hide.

Mireno's budding psychosexual transformation is captured in a sonnet in which he compares himself to a horse whose appetite was initially satisfied by "the green grass of the fields," but once attired in "a gilden harness" it sought greener pastures. So with Mireno, for his courtly garb makes him feel different:

> Mas despertó mi pensamiento noble,
> como al caballo, el cortesano traje:
> que aumenta la soberbia el buen vestido.
> [1.671–74]

> as happens to a horse, my noble thoughts
> were weakened by the touch of courtly cloth:
> thus does fine clothing stoke the sense of pride.

The explicit reference to the horse is suggestive of latent impulses toward the opposite sex which will be awakened when he meets Magdalena in the revitalizing atmosphere of Carnival. And finally, to accord with his change in outward appearance, Mireno takes on a new name, Don Dionís, which will turn out to be his true noble title, although he will not know this until the process of self-integration is comically resolved. Tarso, echoing his master, assumes the pseudonym of Brito.

This fundamental phase of momentary self-loss, confusion, and license is heightened by Tarso's incredible belief that all of those confusions are the work of the enchanter Merlín, Spanish counterpart to the invisible Puck (1.686ff.). Mireno-Dionís and Tarso-Brito are soon mistaken for Ruy Lorenzo and Vasco, respectively, and are carried off as prisoners to the ducal palace. The temporary loss of individual identity is seemingly total, as shown by Tarso's extreme discomfiture with his lackey's garb, especially with his ill-fitting breeches:

> Tarso quiero ser, no Brito;
> ganadero, no lacayo;
> por bragas quiero mi sayo;
> las ollas lloro de Egipto.
> [1.766–69]

> Tarso's for me; of Brito I repent.
> I'd be a rancher, not a serving man;
> give me fine clothes, not these rough pants;
> the tasty foods of Egypt I lament.

The movement toward rediscovery can now begin. Helen Gardner's words with respect to Shakespeare may help to clarify this overall process as it occurs in Tirso: "The trial and error by which we come to knowledge of ourselves and of our world is symbolized by disguisings which are a recurrent element in all comedy, but are particularly common in Shakespeare's. Things have, as it were, to become worse before they become better, more confused and farther from the proper pattern. By misunderstandings men come to understand; and by lies and feignings they discover truth."[10]

Before they separate, Mireno assures Ruy Lorenzo of a haven in the forest with his father Lauro whose innate goodness is a natural extension of his sylvan existence. His own departure, he explains, is motivated not by a desire to abandon his father but by a need to find himself. The forest of Avero, like its counterpart Arden in *As You Like It,* can be seen from varying perspectives.[11] Arden is first of all a natural wilderness capable of producing the vulgarity of the wench Audrey or the gentle simplicity of the shepherd Corin. It is also Arcadia, a pastoral landscape embodied in an ancient and literary tradition which the love affair of Phebe and Silvius represents. At the same time, the forest is the mythic folk place of Robin Hood that offers a corrective for the evils of society and, in particular, the decadence of courtly life. There the banished duke and his "merry men" live and "fleet the time carelessly as they did in the golden world (1.1.115–19)." As the "golden world," Arden reflects a longing for a mythological past age of innocence, security, and sweet fellowship. Addressing his followers as "my comates and brothers in exile" (2.1.1), Duke Senior implies a kind of social equality in the forest environment that he could not know at court. He welcomes the cold of winter because, instead of flattering him as courtiers do, it teaches him the true condition of humankind and of himself (2.1.6–11). But at the same time death through starvation, and even killing for food, are an inevitable part of this sparce forest life. However suitable Arden may be for men like Corin, or however beneficial for others as a temporary haven, Shakespeare does not sentimentalize his vision of pastoral existence: it is not a fit place for all people all the time. While Duke Senior may see "sweetness in adversity" (2.1.12), and while he may learn a great deal from his forced exile, he is aware that it is exile, it is "adversity" and not his proper home. But he neither complains like the fool Touchstone who says, "Ay, now I am in Arden; the more fool I" (2.4.13), nor exaggerates like the melancholy moralist Jaques who carries to extremes the duke's compassion for hunted deer (2.1.26ff.). Whatever the attractions of Arden, it is ultimately a place which all the exiles from court, except one, are only too ready to leave once their former world has been purged of envy and baseness.

The forest of Avero in *El vergonzoso en palacio* can be seen from similar points of view, although the total vision of the pastoral is not as complete as that in *As You Like It*. As a natural wilderness, this forest is equally conducive to the vulgarity of a Tarso and Melisa and to the rustic simplicity of a Bato. Ruy Lorenzo's recent arrival reveals its function as a retreat or haven of the oppressed. The virtues of sylvan existence are exemplified in Lauro, the banished Duke of Coimbra, and bear out the ruminations of the exiled Duke Senior on the sweet uses of adversity. As Ruy's adulation suggests, Lauro incarnates the pastoral ideal of a man untouched by the decadence of courtly life:

> Si la edad y la prudencia
> ofrece en la adversidad,
> Lauro discreto, paciencia,
> vuestra prudencia y edad
> pueden hacer la esperiencia.
>
> [3.1–5]
>
> If age and prudence both dictate
> good Lauro, for adversity
> that patience be the wisest state,
> let your own age and prudence be
> confirmed by showing you can wait.

Lauro's paternal advice on the honorable approach toward vengeance (3.47–53) contrasts sharply with Ruy's shameful act of revenge earlier which resulted, not in the punishment of the guilty Count of Estremoz, but in a treasonous accusation against the innocent Duke of Avero. The pastoral environment thus becomes a corrective for the evils of society. Forest existence, however, is not without its physical dangers and other tribulations; it is the setting of the sportive chase which, considered in its positive aspects, is a suitable diversion among high nobility, but in *El vergonzoso* degenerates into a pernicious (wo)manhunt that manifests itself in a number of ways. Fornoff, for example, suggests that "the hunt for *caza mayor* and *caza menor* [big and small game, 1.89–107] prefigures the pursuit of major and minor alleged traitors (the Duke of Coimbra and Ruy Lorenzo)"; and Weiger argues that the hunt reflects the seduction of Ruy's sister Leonela.[12] Like Arden, the forest of Avero is not a place for everyone at every moment, and those who leave create sadness for those who remain. If the pastoral life enables Lauro to counsel Ruy on the honorable path toward justice, it also makes him grieve at the loss of his own son Mireno (3.224–27). If the decadence and intrigue of the court have contributed to Ruy's inadequate sense of *vergüenza,* or shame, the innocence and sweet fellowship of the forest have imbued Mireno with an exaggerated sense of *vergüenza* or excessive shyness that will inhibit the expression of true feelings of love. Ruy and Mireno are in some way complementary figures, and each must experience a world different from his own in order to achieve a proper balance. Perhaps the underlying connection between the two is signified by their exchange of clothing and by Mireno's arrest in place of Ruy as he tries to leave the forest in search of freedom. Celia's words to the banished Rosalind as they plan their escape from the envious court of Duke Frederick—"Now go we in content / To liberty, and not to banishment" (1.3.133–34)—would seem to apply as well to Mireno, for he is on his way to a Carnival world of license and sanctioned shamelessness where he will discover his true noble status and become integrated both individually and socially.

In his treatment of the pastoral theme in *El vergonzoso,* Tirso reveals a tendency which Jenkins has observed with respect to Shakespeare's comic art, that of "[setting] together the contrasting elements in human nature and [leaving] them by their juxtaposition or interaction to comment on one another."[13] *As You Like It* and *El vergonzoso en palacio* reveal the art of comic juxtaposition at its subtlest in the elaboration of the central love theme. The first encounter between the principal pair of lovers occurs under rather inauspicious circumstances in both plays: Orlando has just been challenged by Duke Frederick's professional wrestler Charles and is about to "try with him the strength of [his] youth" (1.2.160–61); and Mireno, having been accused of abetting the flight of a supposed traitor to the state, is being whisked off to prison within the ducal palace. Rosalind falls in love with the bold and gallant Orlando at first glance, impressed by his having defeated the heretofore invincible Charles (1.3.20). Orlando is no less moved by Rosalind, but however capable he may be of fending for himself materially and physically, he is still rather green spiritually—especially in matters of love. His private confusion becomes apparent as he tries to respond to the young lady's parting words of praise: "What passion hangs these weights upon my tongue?—I cannot speak to her, yet she urg'd conference" (1.2.247–48). At first sight, the duke's daughter Magdalena is similarly impressed by Mireno's seeming courage and inner strength as he is about to be hauled off to prison:

> [*Aparte.*] ¡Estraña audacia
> de hombre! El poco temor

> que muestra dice el valor
> que encubre.
>
> [1.1040–43]
>
> [*Aside.*] What striking courage in
> this man! The total lack of fear
> he shows tells everyone that here
> is a brave man.

Upon hearing his defense of the dishonored man whose garb he has assumed, she is further convinced of his innate worth and hopes for his immediate release (1.1078). Mireno also appears to be taken with Magdalena from the start, for despite his impending incarceration, he feels that fortune has begun to favor him. That he does not express his feelings directly is hardly surprising, but his words to the duke suggest an awareness of having reached a crucial stage in his psychosexual development:

> No soy; seré;
> que sólo por pretender
> ser más de lo que hay en mí
> menosprecié lo que fui
> por lo que tengo de ser.
>
> [1.1035–38]
>
> I'm not; but I will be;
> it is only because I tried
> to surpass what I have inside
> that I despised that once was me
> for the new person you will see.

In the same way that Orlando is immediately welcomed into the forest of Arden by the exiled Duke Senior, who turns out as well to be his father's good friend, so Mireno finds his niche at court upon being pardoned for his transgression and appointed secretary to Magdalena at her request. With physical needs so cared for, and political fears minimized, there is now opportunity for love to flourish. Although it has been virtually love at first sight for these four individuals, in both cases the women take the initiative in maneuvering the love relationship to its logical culmination in marriage.

Orlando, hopelessly smitten by Rosalind but unaware that she is also in Arden disguised as the youth Ganymede, spends his days hanging love poems on trees. Believing that Orlando has been carried away by his protestations of love, Rosalind determines to use her disguise, originally adopted to facilitate her flight from the court, as a means through which to educate the young man in the "proper" attitude toward love. Enumerating the distinguishing marks of a lover (3.2.363ff.), she tells Orlando that he is rather too "point device in [his] accoutrements, as loving [him]self than seeming the lover of any other" (3.2.372–74). Resolving therefore to provide him with a proper sentimental education, "Ganymede" paradoxically proposes a "cure" for the madness caused by his professed love-sickness: he is to pretend that Ganymede is the fair Rosalind and then visit Ganymede's cottage daily to court Ganymede, who will impersonate Rosalind. Orlando agrees but when he is late for his first appointment, Rosalind realizes that whatever her amorous sentiments toward him, she must never allow emotion to overmaster. Nor must she stifle emotion entirely, but properly atone her strong feelings and strike a balance between love and good sense. Orlando does arrive—"within an hour of [his] promise" (4.1.40)—and when his mock wooing is well under way, Ganymede's role perforce changes: she must now direct him away from the excesses of romantic love into which he is now tending and develop in him a deeper, yet constant, response. This she accomplishes in part by exposing love's follies and illusions, especially the erroneous notion that love is an ultimate and final experience, a matter of life and death. "Men have died from time to time and worms have eaten them, but not for love" (4.1.101–3), she tells him. In the mock wedding scene that follows, she becomes convinced by his behavior toward the pretended Rosalind that he loves the real one, and this gives her license to recount the "real" nature of men and women in love, humorously describing not the virtues of marriage but its fallibility: "Men are April when they woo, December when they wed. Maids are May when they are maids, but the sky changes when they are wives" (4.1.139–41). In sum, Ganymede impresses upon Orlando the necessity of keeping his wits about him, even in love, as she herself does. Their common attitude toward love, and to each other, emerges finally as one that, compared with those of the other country couples, bodes best for an enduring relationship. Barber's comments on this process are useful: "Love has been made independent of illusions without becoming any less intense; it is therefore innoculated against life's unromantic contradictions. To emphasize by humor the limitations of the experience has become a way of asserting its reality."[14]

The burgeoning relationship between Magdalena and Mireno is fraught with adventure and inner turmoil, for she has fallen in love with a man who has been led off to prison and whose social rank is unknown:

>     ¿Qué torres sin fundamento
>     tenéis en el aire puestas?
>     ¿Cómo andáis tan descompuestas,
>     imaginaciones locas?
>                                           [2.3–6]
>
>     What flimsy towers have you built
>     foolishly on a base of air?
>     How disordered and unaware
>     can you be, my wild crazy thoughts?

and he is enamored of a noble lady apparently beyond reach:

>     Temerario atrevimiento
>     es el vuestro, pensamiento.
>                                          [2.260–61]
>
>     Oh, my wild thoughts: surely you know
>     what foolish bravado you show.

Magdalena's smitten state contrasts sharply with her earlier attitude of filial submissiveness regarding marriage. Caught as she is between the familiar Baroque conflicts of social convention and passionate feeling ("vergüenza" and "loco apetito"), reason and pleasure ("razón" and "gusto" [2.29–30]), she also realizes that she cannot simply deny her feelings, because

>     ... las llamas tiranas
>     del amor, es cosa cierta
>     que, en cerrándolas la puerta,
>     se salen por las ventanas;
>     cuando les cierren la boca,
>     por los ojos saldrán.
>                                          [2.107–12]
>
>     ... the tyrannical flames
>     of love, a fact you can't ignore,
>     if you lock them behind a door
>     come bursting through the window frames
>     and if you close your mouth to them
>     they'll come shooting out through your eyes.

When Mireno comes before her, the question of his status is uppermost in her mind; his response when asked whether he is "noble" is:

>                  Creo
>     que sí, según lo que veo
>     en mi honrado natural,
>     que muestra más que hay en mí.
>                                          [2.167–69]

> I do believe
> I am, for I know I perceive
> in myself a natural honor
> which shows how much more there is in me.

As Glenn properly observes, "The key to the success of Mireno is his ambition and his self-confidence. He is convinced that he can overcome the restraining force of his humble background, his *naturaleza*. In his conversations with Magdalena . . . he stresses the word *creer:* he believes he is noble."[15] And Magdalena, driven by her love, needs to believe that the external signs of his person—his gentlemanly demeanor and the name Dionís—are the accurate reflection of an inner nobility.

In order to ensure his continued presence at court, she urges him to seek a post as the duke's secretary and so take full advantage of his newfound freedom. Mireno, in trying to make some sense out of the sudden shift from "rags to riches," as it were, attributes Magdalena's intervention on his behalf to her secret love for him:

> ¿No estoy puesto en libertad
> por ella? Y, ya sin enojos,
> por el balcón de sus ojos,
> ¿no he visto su voluntad?
> Amor me tiene.
>
> [2.269–73]

> Am I not placed at liberty
> on her account? And undisguised,
> now, in the windows of her eyes,
> can't I see what she thinks of me?
> She is in love with me.

These fleeting thoughts are largely a projection of his own feelings of love for this noble lady, but on another level, the freedom of which Magdalena and Mireno both speak may be associated with the saturnalian attitude of temporary license and liberty from ordinary limitations which Rosalind reveals during their mock courtship when she says to Orlando, "Come, woo me, woo me; for now I am in a holiday humour and like enough to consent" (4.1.65–66). According to Barber, such holiday humor in Shakespeare's romantic comedies "is often abetted by directly staging pastimes, dances, songs, masques, plays extempore, etc. But the fundamental method is to shape the loose narrative so that 'events' put its persons in the position of festive celebrants: if they do not seek holiday it happens to them. A tyrant duke forces

Rosalind into disguise; but her mock wooing with Orlando amounts to a Disguising, with carnival freedom from the decorum of her identity and her sex."[16] That the main action of *El vergonzoso en palacio* takes place during Carnival is clear proof of the holiday underlying the play. At the ducal palace preparations are under way for the ritual celebration, during which Magdalena's sister Serafina intends to stage a play entitled *La portuguesa cruel*. The roles of the other festive celebrants are not so formally conceived. Mireno's mode of participation bears some resemblance to Rosalind's described above: his disguise as the gentleman Don Dionís provides a form of carnival release from the restrictions of his (apparently) humble identity and his shyness, thereby creating a meaningfully passionate experience that will result in marriage. And Magdalena manifests her holiday humor by temporarily freeing herself from the rules of social decorum and having Mireno appointed her private tutor since the post of secretary has been filled. Overtly Mireno will be offering lessons in the art of writing, whereas covertly she, like her counterpart Rosalind, will be providing lessons in the art of loving.

Having opted for a subtle approach that entails the communication of her lovesick feelings not through words but through nonverbal signs (2.641–62), Magdalena becomes frustrated when Mireno does not appear to be responding to her clear signals of love (2.1081–82). Thus, in an effort to awaken in Mireno pangs of jealousy, thereby shocking him out of his social reticence and *vergüenza*, she feigns love for the Count of Vasconcelos and requests that for her first "lesson" they work at putting these amorous sentiments in writing. This stratagem, however, produces the opposite of its intended effect; Mireno, feeling himself cast in the role of go-between, withdraws even more and chides his mad passion thus:

> ¿Veis, loco amor,
> cuán sin fundamento y fruto
> torre habéis levantado
> de quimeras, que ya han dado
> en el suelo?
>  [2.1114–18]

> Can you not see, foolish love,
> how baselessly and fruitlessly
> you have built towers in the air
> that have come crashing down from there
> to the ground?

He continues to vacillate between sentimental belief and skepticism, but then his strong sense of shame makes him conclude that he is a mere appendage to the favored count Vasconcelos. The lackey Tarso-Brito carries on where Magdalena leaves off, urging his master to take the initiative in matters of love:

> Habla; no pierdas por mudo
> tal mujer y tal estado.
>
> [3.305–6]
>
> Speak up, don't lose from playing dumb
> such a woman and such fine estate.

These words point to the folly of Mireno's excessive *vergüenza*, of the pastoral ideal of innocence and humility, and Tarso's next comment gives the title image to the play:

> No sé yo para qué viene
> el vergonzoso a palacio.
>
> [3.351–52]
>
> I don't know why a bashful man
> here to the palace would have come.

The lackey of course represents the other extreme in the expression of sentiment: he is painfully blunt in telling Melisa that he no longer loves her, saying "Go break other colts. / My soul no longer feels the jolts / of what I once esteemed as love" (domá otros potros; / que ya no me hace quillotros / en el alma vueso amor, 1.184–86); and she is not one to mince her words either, exclaiming, "Is this the way you betray me?" (¿Así me dejas, traidor?, 1.183). Tirso's play, however, is ultimately concerned with establishing a higher plane of communication among lovers that will lead to a clearsighted and sincere relationship; the next interaction between Magdalena and Mireno is intended to facilitate that quest for human understanding in love.

In a climactic burst of holiday humor, Magdalena resolves to declare her love for Mireno openly, flouting the norms of the collective; she will resort to the stratagem of pretending to be asleep and dreaming aloud.[17] This ruse serves a function similar to that of Rosalind's disguise as Ganymede: it affords her freedom from the decorum of social convention and the opportunity for authentic communication. Magdalena's simulated dream sequence is virtually a mini play-within-a-play, and Mireno is spectator of the illusion. Only later will he be asked to assume the part of actor or participant and reenact the contents of the "dream," thereby becoming a festive celebrant not unlike Magdalena, Rosalind, and Orlando. Mireno's initial response to the "sleeping beauty" smacks of the exaggerations of conventional sentiment which Tirso is presumably intending to deflate:

> ¿Hizo el Autor soberano
> de nuestra naturaleza
> más acabada belleza?
> Besarla quiero una mano.
> ¿Llegaré? Sí; pero no;
> que es la reliquia divina,
> y mi humilde boca, indina
> de tocalla.
>
> [3.473–80]

> How can the Creator have planned
> in all of nature's artifice
> a beauty more perfect than this?
> I want to go and kiss her hand.
> Shall I approach her? Yes; but no;
> She's a relic of divine love,
> and my crude mouth unworthy of
> ever touching her.

Such Petrarchist idealism—which views the woman as a beautiful object to be passively worshipped from afar rather than actively and authentically engaged as a human being—may explain Mireno's sudden impulse to depart and Magdalena's resultant imprecation: "Oh confound such bashfulness!" (¡Mal haya tanta vergüenza!, 3.492). Mireno returns almost immediately, but he continues to invoke Petrarchist imagery in his speech:

> Obedecella es razón,
> pues, aunque duerme, es mi dueño.
>
> [3.511–12]

> Reason says to obey her still,
> for though she sleeps, she's still my lord.

Magdalena carries her dream sequence one step further by playing both parts in a "dialogic monolgue" between Mireno and his "secret mistress" or, as it were, between two opposing parts of himself. Since her purpose is to facilitate the clear and uninhibited expression of unspoken feelings and desires, she begins by saying that flattering glances are as frustrating and ineffectual as jumbled speech (3.550ff.). In the same way that Orlando's initial innocence stems, not from temperament but from a poor "education," so Mireno's "vergüenza" is the result of fears and anxieties—generated by inflexible social norms and moral standards—which must be dissipated if he is ever to have a deeply felt and untainted love experience. Equality of rank does not make for authenticity in love; rather love grows out of mutual concern and desire ("la conformidad / del alma y la voluntad" [3.602–3]). Once she has exercised her own will and stated explicitly her preference for "Don Dionís" over the Count Vasconcelos, Magdalena "awakens" and asks the bemused Mireno to recount what has happened so as to assess the impact of her words. Her overt expression of annoyance at his continued reticence finally shocks him into verbalizing the key point of the dialogue, namely that she feels affection for him and even prefers him to Vasconcelos (3.660–64). Although Magdalena in a moment of frustration then denies the validity of anything spoken "in dreams" ("que los sueños, sueños son" [3.668]), and although Mireno thinks only of the simplicity of his former existence in contrast to the intrigues of the palace, they both have reached the point where a love affair between them is potentially possible. Magdalena's simulated dialogue is functionally similar to Rosalind's mock wooing and wedding scene: each heroine has engaged her lover in an educational process described by Frye as a "movement from illusion to reality," from "a society controlled by habit, ritual bondage, arbitrary law and the older characters to a society controlled by youth and pragmatic freedom."[18] Magdalena and Mireno quickly come to know the advantages of such "pragmatic freedom" when, during another "lesson," the duke suddenly announces that his daughter is to be given in marriage to Vasconcelos the very next day. Magdalena throws caution to the wind and writes(!) Mireno a note inviting him to a night assignation in the garden (perhaps that "green world" of ritual where spring and summer triumph over winter). Mireno is finally able to overcome his inhibitions and openly rejoice at the intended liaison:

> Presto en tu florido espacio
> dará envidia entre mis celos,
> al conde de Vasconcelos,
> *El vergonzoso en palacio.*
>
> [3.1198–1201]

> Soon in your flowery place I can
> present that Vasconcelos count
> envy that jealousy surmounts
> of the palace's bashful man.

Magdalena and Mireno, paralleling Rosalind and Orlando, have come to a serious understanding in love that, combined with the discovery of the hero's true parentage and social status, and compared with the attitudes toward love of the other couples, augurs well for an enduring relationship.

Barber has stated that the best analogies for the structure of *As You Like It* are in music; the musical analogy is also applicable to *El vergonzoso en palacio*. Shakespeare's play, according to Barber, is composed in two movements, the first developing the pastoral theme, and the second the romantic.[19] Once Rosalind finds Orlando's verses at the beginning of act 3, the rest of the play's second movement elaborates variations on the theme of love. The triple love affairs of the hero and heroine, Silvius and Phebe, Touchstone and Audrey, succeed one another while the dramatist plays each off against the others through the techniques of parallel and parody. If Rosalind and Orlando represent the most balanced attitude toward love, theirs has been defined in part by the relationships of other lovers. At one extreme, the pastoral pair Silvius and Phebe reveal how the exaggerated sentiment of the Petrarchist tradition may subvert the sincere expression of love. (We have already seen how Orlando, especially when he takes to hanging verses upon trees, tends toward these excesses until checked by Rosalind and how Mireno engages in similar antics when he worships the "sleeping" Magdalena during her simulated dream sequence.) Silvius and Phebe depict the hyperbole of conventional sentiment in a brief courting scene which is presented almost as a formal spectacle ("a pageant truly play'd" [3.4.48]), with the shepherd Corin for director and Rosalind and her cousin Celia for audience. What we witness along with the inner stage public is played "truly" according to the best literary tradition: Silvius begs not to be scorned, and Phebe responds with disdain, refusing to believe in the invisible wounds made by "love's keen arrows" (3.5.30–31). The disguised Rosalind-Ganymede interrupts their pageant, reminding them that as nature's "ordinary" creatures, they should refrain from extreme forms of amorous liking or spurning: to the lovesick Silvius she says, "You foolish shepherd, wherefore do you follow her / Like foggy South puffing with wind and rain?"; and to the disdainful Phebe, "Sell when you can, you are not for all markets" (3.5.42, 49–50, 60). Rosalind's excessive frankness here underscores the excesses of conventional sentiment, but these antics are satirized principally through the device of having Phebe fall in love with the "boy Ganymede."

At the opposite extreme from Silvius and Phebe, and therefore no closer to a balanced view (although they help to define that view) are Touchstone, the court fool who has followed Rosalind into exile, and the country wench Audrey. Touchstone's affair with Audrey degrades love by reducing it to the lowest common denominator of sensual gratification, without any sentiment at all: "As the ox hath his bow, sir, . . . so man hath his desires" (3.3.71–72). The viewpoint is of course the reverse of Petrarchist idealism, where the lover is first overcome by the beauty of his mistress, then incited by that beauty to value and desire her. Touchstone, however, places desire before beauty and attraction, as suggested by his plans to be united to Audrey, not by a priest in church but by the country vicar Sir Oliver Martext, in what would be fundamentally a false match. Only the timely intervention of the melancholy satirist Jaques prevents their being joined together "as they join wainscot" (3.3.78), although in an aside Touchstone says he would prefer it that way: "Not being well married, it will be a good excuse for me hereafter to leave my wife" (3.3.83–85). But he will take his place "amongst the other country copulatives," as he puts it, and he tells his bride-to-be, "Come sweet Audrey, / —We must be married or we must live in bawdry" (3.3.87–88). However detached and objective Touchstone's perspective, and clear-sighted his acknowledgment of his need for self-gratification, the fact is that he reflects only a partial attitude toward love. Touchstone's degradation of love complements the exaggerated sentimental display of Silvius and Phebe. According to Barber, these "two polar attitudes which are balanced against each other in the action as a whole, meet and are reconciled in Rosalind's personality. Because she remains always aware of love's illusions while she herself is swept along by its deepest currents, she possesses as an attribute of character the power of combining wholehearted feeling and undistorted judgment."[20]

In *El vergonzoso en palacio*, the *gracioso*-lackey Tarso, like the court fool Touchstone, provides the comic commentary on the serious action, especially with respect to the theme of love. His aborted affair with Melisa is intended as a parody of romantic love in that it degrades the value of sentiment. His response to his former mistress's complaint of abandonment reveals a priority of desire and instinct to true attraction and feeling that smacks of Touchstone's own viewpoint:

> Melisa: domá otros potros;
> que ya no me hace quillotros

> en el alma vueso amor.
> Con la ausencia de medio año
> que ha que ni os busco ni os veo,
> curó el tiempo mi deseo,
> la enfermedad de un engaño.
>
> [1.184–90]
>
> Melissa, go break other colts.
> My soul no longer feels the jolts
> of what I once esteemed as love.
> In the half year I've been away
> and neither sought nor thought of you
> time cured me; my desire is through,
> your sick deceits faded away.

In the end, Tarso's marriage to Melisa is every bit as forced as Touchstone's union with Audrey. In the one case, Jaques tells Touchstone, "Get you to church, and have a good priest that can tell you what marriage is" (3.3.75–76). And in the other, Melisa, although she persists in calling Tarso a fickle, ungrateful traitor ("traidor, mudable, ingrato" [3.1640]), beseeches Mireno (who by this time has discovered his true identity as Don Dionís) to arrange not only their marriage but their love. Don Dionís not only acquiesces in her plea, but promises Tarso financial compensation if he consents. It would seem, then, that Tarso's reasons for marrying are just as degrading and humiliating as Touchstone's, for he is presumably motivated by material (rather than physical) desire and untouched by sentiment of any kind. Neither bonding bodes well; Jaques's prediction that Touchstone's and Audrey's marriage will be fraught with "wrangling," and "is but for two months victuall'd" (5.4.190–91), is equally applicable to the Tirsian pair. The effect of having Tarso illustrate what in love is unromantic is not, however, to undercut the romantic victory of Mireno and Magdalena in the play. Rather the lackey, moved as he is by desire—whether physical or material—and not by sentiment, serves as a foil to the hero by exposing the follies of pastoral humility and innocence—*vergüenza*—(3.291ff.), and consequently spurs him on in his amorous conquest of the heroine. Furthermore, Tarso's mockery of any and all sentiment in his own love affair provides a counterstatement to the exaggerated sentimentality of the Petrarchist tradition, toward which Mireno tends initially when he expresses his feelings for Magdalena during her feigned dream (3.509ff.), and which the smitten Antonio abuses in his pursuit of the disdainful Serafina.

Antonio falls madly in love when he first sees the younger

daughter of the Duke of Avero, whom he perceives wholly in terms of conventional imagery:

> bella es doña Magdalena,
> pero doña Serafina
> es el sol de Portugal.
> Por la vista el alma bebe
> llamas de amor entre nieve,
> por el vaso de cristal
> de su divina blancura:
> la fama ha quedado corta
> en su alabanza.
>
> [1.914–22]

> Doña Magdalena is fine,
> but Doña Serafina is
> Portugal's sun that shines so bright.
> The soul imbibes what the eyes show:
> fiery flames from among the snow
> in a crystal goblet, so white
> its purity must be divine.
> Her fame I fear has fallen short
> in the praises it sings of her.

If at first Antonio, in his impassioned pursuit of the scornful Serafina recalls the all-suffering Silvius, he soon proves to be a courtly inversion, if not perversion, of the pastoral ideal. Although Antonio is moved by the beauty of his "adored seraphim" (2.368), he resorts to ignoble subterfuge to achieve his goal of reciprocity in love: he abandons his plans to serve the Castilian King Juan II and solicits, with the aid of his cousin Juana (who is also lady to Serafina), the post of secretary to the Duke of Avero despite her (Juana's) comment about the inappropriateness of his action. Like Mireno, he disguises his true self, but, unlike the hero, he feigns an identity which, while close to his own, is nonetheless socially beneath it—that of servant to himself, to one Antonio de Barcelos, Count of Penela (2.432). Mireno, on the other hand, moves upward on the social ladder and impersonates the noble Don Dionís who turns out to be the person he really is. Glenn's assessment of the contrasting motives of the two men stresses this point: "The masquerade of Antonio . . . is so different from that of Mireno, though both are serving in the same position. Mireno brings credit to himself in his new identity whereas Antonio is shameless."[21]

Serafina, like Antonio, is also given to disguise and role-playing but in a more formal way; she characteristically assumes the parts of young men in fictional dramatizations—although professing to despise men in "real" life—and is currently rehearsing a part for the approaching festivities of Carnival. Her own description of her intended representation suggests that her role-playing is not simply play-acting but rather an unconscious expression of psychosexual fantasies; there is implicit from the start an unnatural conflation of self and role:

> Deséome entretener
> deste modo; no te asombre
> que apetezca el traje de hombre,
> ya que no lo puedo ser.
> [2.735–38]

> This is the manner that I plan
> to amuse myself; don't take fright
> if men's clothes whet my appetite,
> though I can't truly be a man.

In her capacity as detached commentator, Juana prophetically verbalizes her concern to Serafina who unabashedly gazes upon herself in a looking glass:

> Si te miras
> en [el espejo], ten, señora, aviso,
> no te enamores de ti. . . .
> Temo que has de ser Narciso.
> [2.802–4,806]

> If you look at yourself
> in the mirror, my lady, take care
> you do not fall in love with yourself. . . .
> I fear that you will be Narcissus.

While Serafina is thus possessed by her own reflection, a concealed painter is simultaneously observing her image so as to mirror it on a canvas for the self-indulgent and impassioned Antonio, who is himself hidden and watching the two artists at work—as we spectators look upon the entire spectacle from without. This is, as Fornoff says, "a splendid example of art reflecting art reflecting reality,"[22] and the concentric circles of illusion will become even more labyrinthine as soon as Serafina begins rehearsing the part of a spurned prince who, overwrought by feelings of love and jealousy for one Celia, threatens a rival count with death (2.869–96). Juana, from her vantage point outside the action, comments upon the seeming parallels between the unloving character of the disdainful Portuguese lady and Serafina's narcissistic personality—parallels which the actress professes not to notice. Once the rehearsal is under way, Juana is forced to interrupt the action a number of times—thereby causing inner illusion to merge with outer "reality"—and chide her mistress for becoming overly impassioned in her dramatic interpretation and allowing the play almost to run away with her. Serafina's potentially destructive propensity to over(re)act and lose herself in her role is heightened when, in the midst of her impersonation of the jealous prince, she unconsciously breaks the illusion by embracing the startled Juana and professing her love. Juana, however, maintains her distance and poses the following key question:

> ¿es posible que quien siente
> y hace así un enamorado
> no tenga amor?
>
> [2.947–48]
>
> Can it be true that one who feels
> and plays the lover in this way
> is not in love?

Serafina is indeed capable of loving, but only of loving herself to a pathological degree. Her impersonations have caused her to play out negative aspects of her personality of which she does not seem to be aware. Her narcissistic tendencies stand in direct opposition to Magdalena's strong desire to share herself with another. Gardner, we recall, has remarked that "by misunderstandings men come to understand; and by lies and feignings they discover truth." All four individuals—Mireno and Magdalena, Antonio and Serafina—engage in some form of role-playing and/or disguise: only in the case of the first pair, however, does fiction lead to self-discovery and to mutual understanding in love (paralleling the experience of Orlando and Rosalind); whereas in the second instance, illusion limits authentic self-realization and the sincere expression of human emotion.

The thematic content of *La portuguesa cruel* not only echoes the ridiculous (if not perverse) expression of conventional sentiment exhibited by Silvius and Phebe, but it also prefigures the counterproductive antics of Antonio and Serafina in the "real" world of Tirso's fiction. Antonio, having been spurned by an outraged Serafina once she learns of his deceit, pronounces all the excesses of jealousy and unrequited love:

> Aspid, que entre las rosas
> desa belleza escondes tu veneno,

> ¿mis quejas amorosas
> desprecias deste modo?
>
> [3.762–65]

> Serpent, who secretly lies
> among this beauty's roses with your fangs,
> tell me: how can you despise
> this way my lover's complaints?

In contrast to his pastoral counterpart Silvius who, following literary tradition, asks pity of his scornful mistress—"Will you sterner be / Than he that dies and lives by bloody drops" (3.5.6–7)—Antonio, already jaded by the "envious court," plots revenge against the rejecting Serafina:

> Pues que del paraíso
> de su vista destierras mi ventura,
> hágate amor Narciso,
> y de tu misma imagen y hermosura
> de suerte te enamores,
> que, como llora, sin remedio llores.
>
> [3.768–73]

> Since your cruelty dismisses
> me from the paradise of seeing you
> may love make of you Narcissus,
> so when the image of yourself you view
> your beauty wounds you so deep
> that, as I weep, bereft of hope you weep.

Serafina, for her part, echoes the tryannical Phebe in her ironical negation of love's power to affect her life:

> ¡Dichosa mil veces yo,
> que jamás admití el yugo
> de tan tirano verdugo!
>
> [3.802–4]

> How greatly fortunate I am
> that in my life I've never choked
> on that executioner's yoke!

The moment she pronounces these words, she spies the self-portrait which Antonio has abandoned in conscious pursuit of revenge. Tirso satirizes these excesses of conventional sentiment through the device of having Serafina fall in love with her own image sketched while she was rehearsing in masculine costume. She is immediately ensnared by the reproducton of her own likeness which she does not recognize, presumably because the color of the garb has changed from black to a combination of gold and blue (colors already associated with love and jealousy in Antonio's initial reference to the rival Count Estremoz, as Casalduero has pointed out).[23] Juana at once notes the supreme irony in the unexpected turn of events:

> [*Ap.*] ¡Hay más singular
> suceso! Castigo ha sido
> del cielo que a su retrato
> ame quien a nadie amó.
>
> [3.888–91]
>
> Can there have been a stranger
> happenstance? It's a punishment
> of God that one who never loved
> anyone her portrait should love.

Tirso's use of conventional technique here, resulting in what Serafina herself calls a "strange confusion" (3.837–38), clearly parallels Shakespeare's device of having Phebe become enamored of Rosalind disguised as the boy Ganymede. But by making Serafina fall in love with her own image, and not with that of generic woman, Tirso lays stress on her inherent narcissism, also brought out when she gazed upon her image in the looking glass before starting to rehearse *La portuguesa cruel* (2.805ff.)

Frye states that the typical structure of Shakespearean comedy may best be apprehended by recalling three elements present in the ritual forms preceding drama: (1) the somber period of preparation represented, for example by the Christian Lent, where there is an attempt to recognize and eliminate the principle of sterility later identified with sin and evil; (2) the period of license and confusion of values symbolized by the carnival, the saturnalia, and the festivals of promiscuous sexual union that appear in early religions; (3) the period of festivity itself, the revel or *komos* which is said to have given its name to comedy.[24] Shakespearean comic structure normally reproduces these three aspects of ritual form in the order outlined here, and *As You Like It* is no exception. Tirsian comedy, as exemplified by *El vergonzoso en palacio*, follows a similar overall pattern.

The first structural phase reveals an anticomic society—a social organization blocking and opposed to the comic drive—which the action of the play evades or overcomes. The obstructing forces frequently take the form of a harsh or irrational law that is concerned mostly with regulating the sexual drive and so works against the wishes of the hero and heroine, which form the main thrust of the comic action. In *As You Like It,* this law is simultaneously personified in the humorous Duke Frederick, whose tyrannical will is law, and in the jealous Oliver, who treats his brother Orlando with utter contempt. In *El vergonzoso,* parallel blocking forces coexist at various levels: politically in the treason that is responsible for both Lauro's exile and Mireno's loss of (noble) identity; socially in the treachery that brings dishonor to Ruy Lorenzo's sister and to himself; and paternally in the Duke of Avero's attempt to marry off his daughters to the Counts Vasconcelos and Estremoz against their will. The second phase of comic structure is one of temporarily lost identity, confusion, and sexual license, which is portrayed principally through the device of impenetrable disguise; consistent with the main theme of comedy, this loss of identity is most often a loss of sexual identity. In Shakespeare, Rosalind's disguise as the boy Ganymede and her wooing of the "unbred" Orlando (1.1.4) in the forest of Arden symbolize this period of alienation and confusion. In Tirso, Mireno's dominant *vergüenza* and lack of "breeding," his (ex)change of clothing and impersonation of the noble Don Dionís, and Magdalena's resultant feignings on the eve of Carnival all signalize this stage (echoed negatively in Serafina's play-acting and Antonio's dissimulations).

The third and final phase of comedy is concerned with the discovery of identity.[25] The most common form of identity is that achieved by marriage, where two fleshes become one and, in Hymen's apt phrase, "atone together" (5.4.109). The erotic center of the comic drive toward identity is often represented by an Eros figure who effects the comic conclusion but is himself sexually self-contained, needing no expression of love beyond himself; the heroine disguised as a boy also fulfills this bisexual Eros role. In *As You Like It,* Rosalind's sexual disguise and her eventual repossession of her normal female garments—or, put another way, her disappearance and her return—bring about the birth of a new society and the reconciliation of the older one with it. While the overriding theme of the comic is the rejuvenation of society, a prior and necessary step is the integration of the individual. Singular identity occurs when a person comes to know her/himself in a way s/he did not before: comedy, as Frye says, "is designed not to condemn evil, but to ridicule a lack of self-knowledge."[26]

Rosalind culminates this dual process of self-discovery and social regeneration by pretending to have a magician uncle who will perform the final metamorphoses. The sudden betrothal of Celia and Oliver (who has been converted to goodness in Arden's sylvan environment) provides the impetus for the comic *anagnorisis* that results in the quadruple wedding ceremony.[27] The controlling society of the earlier part of the play—with its irrational laws, jealousies, and tyrannical whims—is dissolved and a new society crystalizes around the marriage of the central figures Orlando and Rosalind, incorporating as many other people as possible. Oliver's transformation and Duke Frederick's timely conversion by a saintly hermit, with the happy result that Duke Senior is restored to his proper place in society, are designed to make the comic world in the end as inclusive as it can be. There are nevertheless two characters who remain isolated from the action, spectators of it, and as such identifiable with the spectator aspect of ourselves. The fool Touchstone, in his special capacity as commentator on human folly, exists outside the realm of ordinary experience. He is prevented from sharing in the human love and conciliation with which the play ends, and although he marries, his marriage is a mere mockery of the institution rather than a serious attempt at commitment. Jaques, whom Frye terms the *idiotes*, is "simply opposed by temperament to festivity."[28] A detached spectator and critic of the action, he remains forever committed to a view of life as a meaningless process of decay, governed by inexorable time (which his "Seven Ages of Man" speech is meant to show [2.7.139ff.]). When the duke is restored to his former position, Jaques does not join in the dance which celebrates the new order of the lovers. But having seen them all endure "shrewd days and nights" (5.4.172), he accepts this as evidence of their inner worth, and perhaps for the first time in the play, sees hope of order, not of disorder. He speaks formally first to the duke:

> You to your former honour I bequeath,
> Your patience and your virtue well deserve it;

and then to Orlando, Oliver, and Silvius in turn:

> You to a love that your true faith doth merit:
> You to your land and love and great allies:
> You to a long and well-deserved bed.
>
> [5.4.185–89]

But for Touchstone, he foresees "wrangling"; the jester's "loving voyage / Is but for two months victuall'd" (5.4.190–91). Jaques thus provides a rational and detached appraisal of these couples' several chances of achieving true love in the more complex world that is their society.

Prior to the comic discovery of identity in *El vergonzoso en palacio,* there is a final descent into extreme confusion precipitated by the night assignation which Magdalena and Serafina have arranged, each of whom has asked a man named "Dionís" to appear in the garden at precisely the same moment. Magdalena's invitation to Mireno-Dionís is a logical outgrowth of the temporary license of Carnival—in Barber's words, "a 'misrule' which implied rule"[29]—and is an expression of true feelings of love. Serafina, on the other hand, bases her proposed liaison on a blatant lie: Antonio, having been pressed into revealing the origin of the portrait which he has purposefully abandoned, has invented a tale that closely parallels the "real" history of Mireno-Dionís, with the addition that the latter is deeply in love with Serafina but, because of his father's exile, could not appear to woo her lest he be considered a traitor. Antonio, therefore, has "generously" made the portrait available so that Serafina may fall in love with her secret admirer. Using words such as "lie" (3.908, 944) and "deception" (3.925), he speaks frankly to Juana of what he perceives to be an elaborate falsehood:

> Ni sé del duque, ni dónde
> su hijo y mujer llevó.
> Don Dionís he de ser yo
> de noche, y de día el conde
> de Penela; y desta suerte,
> si amor su ayuda me da,
> mi industria me entregará
> lo que espero.
>
> [3.1082–89]

> I don't know of the duke, nor where
> he went with his son, or his wife.
> Now at night I will live the life
> of Dionís, and by day's glare
> count Penela; thus in this way,
> if Love gives me the help I need,
> my ingenuity will cede me what I want.

Tirso has succeeded in blurring the lines that separate fiction and reality, story and history, and Antonio becomes a *burlador burlado* (deceiver turned deceived) when the illusion he has invented turns out to be virtually true. The major difference between Magdelena and Serafina, then, is that the former arrives at truth through love and conversely learns to love truly, whereas the latter continues to embrace falsehood and be estranged from real human sentiments. Robert ter Horst sees Antonio's true lie and Serafina's false belief as playing a crucial role in the self-realization of Mireno-Dionís: "Serafina believes in Dionís on the strength of life image alone. To be true, a faith must be falsifiable. Don Antonio's Dionís attests to the veracity of Mireno's Dionís. One [version] is authentic and the other false. The authentic version profits when the false one is exposed."[30]

The discovery of individual identity and the accompanying restitution of social order in *El vergonzoso en palacio* is catalyzed by the unexpected announcement that the Portuguese King Alfonso Quinto has restored the confiscated lands and wealth to the rightful Duke of Coimbra, alias the shepherd Lauro, but once again a loyal and noble subject (3.1443), as well as ordered the punishment of the traitorous Vasco Fernández. Mireno assumes his true noble title as Don Dionís, thereby acquiring a social status equal to that of Magdalena. Antonio confesses that he has shamefully deceived Serafina by impersonating Don Dionís and usurping the identity of another. The Counts Vasconcelos and Estremoz are unable to claim their promised brides Magdalena and Serafina, both of whom are otherwise committed—the one out of true love to the rightful Don Dionís, and the other out of false infatuation to the deceitful Antonio, Count of Penela. The Duke of Avero, who has functioned all along as a paternal blocking figure concerning the marriage of his daughters, now approves their self-arranged matches—most willingly in Magdalena's case and rather reluctantly in Serafina's. Ruy Lorenzo, having accompanied the Duke of Coimbra out of exile, is still in need of someone to right *his* wrongs; he finally receives satisfaction when the usurping Count Estremoz offers to remedy his affront to Leonela by marrying her. Melisa wins her Tarso, but, like Touchstone, the lackey will marry without any serious commitment to marriage and continue to exist outside the realm of ordinary human responses. Juana is not a part of the wedding festivities, although the Duke of Avero promises her a worthy husband (3.1655). That she stands aloof in the end is not surprising, for in her dual capacity as cousin to Antonio and lady to Serafina, she has served throughout as a detached spectator and commentator on the dramatic action and is thus identifiable with the spectator aspect of ourselves.

In the same manner as their Shakespearean counterparts, these

Tirsian couples have varying chances of finding fulfillment in their newly acquired social alliances; Hymen's ceremonious words to Orlando and Rosalind, Phebe, and Touchstone and Audrey would seem to be equally applicable, respectively, to Mireno and Magdalena, Serafina, and Tarso and Melisa:

> You and you no cross shall part. . . .
> You to his love must accord,
> Or have a woman to your lord.
> You and you are sure together,
> As the winter to foul weather..
> [5.4.130, 132–35]

In Shakespeare as in Tirso, then, marriage is affirmed as an institution, although *not* the perfect solution for all. Barber's words concerning the festive experiment in As You Like It are worth noting here, *alternative* approaches to the Shakespeare canon notwithstanding.[31]

> In dramatizing love's intensity as the release of a festive moment, Shakespeare keeps that part of the romantic tradition which makes love an experience of the whole personality, even though he ridicules the wishful absolutes of doctrinaire romantic love. He does not found his comedy on the sort of saturnalian simplification which equates love with sensual gratification. He includes spokesmen for this sort of release in reduction; but they are never given an unqualified predominance, though they contribute to the atmosphere of liberty within which the aristocratic lovers find love. It is the latter who hold the balance near the center.[32]

And so with Tirso in the creation of his festive comedy, where opposing views of love are seemingly reconciled and balanced in the principal pairs of lovers, but where the perspective on life and love, so multifariously conceived and evolved, also entreats the spectator (and reader/critic)—as Rosalind puts it in the epilogue—"to like as much of this play as please [them]" (5.4.210–11). By so encouraging the search for multiplicity of meaning, these Shakespearean and Tirsian texts defy being reduced to a set of monolithic structures based on the spectator's, the reader's, the critic's, or the author's preconceived notions of life and love.

## Notes

This article owes its existence to the uninterrupted time and inspirational theatrical milieu I was able to enjoy at the Stratford Shakespearean Festival of Canada and, in particular, to the Festival's 1983 production of *As You Like It*, directed by John Hirsch. I am grateful to Bucknell University for providing a Faculty Development Grant which allowed me to take full advantage of that opportunity. I also wish to thank David M. Gitlitz for his rendition of Tirso's Spanish verse into English.

1. Margaret Wilson, *Tirso de Molina* (Boston: Twayne, 1977), p. 48. Tirsian comedy in general, and *El vergonsozo en palacio* in particular, have suffered from the same sort of critical shortsightedness that hampered an appreciation of Shakespearean comedy and romance. See Northrop Frye, *A Natural Perspective: The Development of Shakespearean Comedy and Romance* (New York: Harcourt, Brace & World, 1965), p. 6. Nevertheless, in the past two decades, *El vergonzoso* has received some of the critical attention it deserves. See, for example, Joaquín Casalduero, "Sentido y forma de *El vergonzoso en palacio*," *Nueva Revista de Filología Hispánica* 15 (1961): 198–216; Richard F. Glenn, "Disguises and Masquerades in Tirso's *El vergonzoso en palacio*," *Bulletin of the Comediantes* 17 (1965): 16–22; Ion Tudor Agheana, *The Situational Drama of Tirso de Molina* (Madrid: Playor, 1973), pp. 73–80; David H. Darst, *The Comic Art of Tirso de Molina* (Chapel Hill, N.C.: Estudios de Hispanófila, 1974); Frederick H. Fornoff, "Symbolic Action in Tirso's *El vergonzoso en palacio*," *Revista Hispánica Moderna* 39 (1976–77): 39–48; Everett W. Hesse, "La imaginación creadora en *El vergonzoso en palacio*," in *Interpretando la comedia* (Madrid: Porrúa, 1977), pp. 55–70; Robert ter Horst, "Experienced Innocence: Tirso's *El vergonzoso en palacio*," *Kentucky Romance Quarterly* 25 (1978): 129–43; John G. Weiger, "La pertinencia del primer cuadro de *El vergonzoso en palacio*," in *Perspectivas de la comedia*, ed. Alva V. Ebersole (Valencia: Albatros, 1979), 2:93–102; Ann E. Wiltrout, "Mileno, Mireno: Creation and Character in *El vergonzoso en palacio*," *Bulletin of the Comediantes* 35 (1983): 189–95; Raymond Conlon, "Female Psychosexuality in Tirso's *El vergonzoso en palacio*," *Bulletin of the Comediantes* 37 (1985): 55–69.

2. Bruce W. Wardropper, "La comedia española del Siglo de Oro," in Elder Olson, *Teoría de la comedia* (Barcelona: Ariel, 1978), pp. 195, 209–15.

3. C. L. Barber, *Shakespeare's Festive Comedy: A Study of Dramatic Form and Its Relation to Social Custom* (Princeton: Princeton University Press, 1959), p. 4. Chapter 9, "The Alliance of Seriousness and Levity in *As You Like It*," appeared in slightly different form as "The Use of Comedy in *As You Like It*," in *Philological Quarterly* 21 (1942): 353–67; reprinted in *Twentieth-Century Interpretations of* As You Like It: *A Collection of Critical Essays*, ed. Jay Halio (Englewood Cliffs, N.J.: Prentice Hall, 1968), pp. 14–27.

4. William Shakespeare, *As You Like It*, ed. Agnes Latham, Arden edition (London: Methuen, 1975), 1.1.115–19. For a survey of traditional scholarly thought on *As You Like It*, see Latham's introduction, pp. ix–xcv.

5. In his insightful study of the phallic implications of the conventional imagery pertaining to the honor code in *El vergonzoso en palacio*, Fornoff attaches considerable importance to the Carnival atmosphere underlying the play's action: "Tirso causally links [the] psychological integration of the individual to the reintegration of a disturbed society by presenting the initiation rites of the individual in a Carnival setting. The festive movement from chaos to order during Carnival coincides with Mireno's movement from confusion to self-discovery" ("Symbolic Action," p. 39). Fornoff's analysis, however, limits itself to only one aspect of the multifaceted vision of Eros which Tirso's play provides.

6. Terry Eagleton, *William Shakespeare* (Oxford: Blackwell, 1986), pp. 90–91. For a balanced overview of the deconstructionist method, see Christopher Norris, *Deconstruction: Theory and Practice* (London: Methuen, 1982); and for an exposition of new directions in Shakespeare criticism (e.g., Marxism, new historicism, feminism, deconstruction), including specific reference to *As You Like It*, see John Drakakis, ed. *Alternative Shakespeares* (London: Methuen, 1985).

7. All references to *El vergonzoso en palacio* are given, by act and verse, from the Clásicos castellanos edition by Américo Castro (Madrid: Espasa-Calpe, 1922). English translations of Tirso's verse are by David M. Gitlitz.

8. Bruce W. Wardropper, in "Comic Illusion: Lope de Vega's *El perro del hortelano*," *Kentucky Romance Quarterly* 14 (1967), says that "in problematic, or fundamentally serious, plays, the illusoriness of man's world is usually made apparent in the opening scene" (p. 101); Weiger, in "La pertinencia," has shown this to be the case in his detailed analysis of the opening scenes of *El vergonzoso en palacio*.

9. Frye, *A Natural Perspective*, p. 76.

10. Helen Gardner, *"As You Like It,"* in Halio, ed., *Critical Essays*, p. 65. More recently, Walter Cohen has argued from a Marxist perspective that when characters in romantic comedy don a disguise and engage in acting that leads to mistaken identities, the improbable situations they must confront not only signal the failure of the predominant social code ("the simultaneous instability and rigidity of the ruling class's position"), but they also designate preferred alternatives to the imposed constraints of daily life: "Pastoral, intrigue, lower-class disguise, acting, the atmosphere of holiday or of release—all testify to a utopian impulse toward freedom and an extended range of self-expression." See *Drama of a Nation: Public Theatre in Renaissance England and Spain* (Ithaca: Cornell University Press, 1985), p. 189.

11. In addition to essays by Barber and Gardner already cited, the following two studies are representative of those that provide insight into the complex nature of Arden: Harold Jenkins, *"As You Like It,"* in Halio, ed., *Critical Essays*, pp. 28–43; and David Young, *The Heart's Forest: A Study of Shakespeare's Pastoral Plays* (New Haven: Yale University Press, 1972), pp. 38–72.

12. Fornoff, "Symbolic Action," p. 41, and Weiger, "La pertinencia," p. 97.

13. Jenkins, *"As You Like It,"* p. 33.

14. Barber, *Festive Comedy*, p. 236.

15. Glenn, "Disguises and Masquerades," p. 19.

16. Barber, *Festive Comedy*, p. 6.

17. See Agheana's discussion of Tirso's experimentation with such "dialogic monologic sequences" in *The Situational Drama of Tirso de Molina*, pp. 73–80.

18. Northrop Frye, *Anatomy of Criticism* (New York: Atheneum, 1968), p. 169.

19. Barber, "Use of Comedy," in Halio, ed., *Critical Essays*, pp. 18–19.

20. Barber, *Festive Comedy*, p. 233.

21. Glenn, "Disguises and Masquerades," p. 18.

22. Fornoff, "Symbolic Action," p. 48.

23. Casalduero, "Sentido y forma," p. 207.

24. Frye, *A Natural Perspective*, p. 73.

25. Ibid., pp. 78–85, passim.

26. Northrop Frye, "The Argument of Comedy," in *English Institute Essays*, ed. D. A. Robertson, Jr. (New York: Columbia University Press, 1949), p. 61.

27. Frye, *Anatomy of Criticism*, p. 163.

28. Frye, *A Natural Perspective*, p. 93.

29. Barber, *Festive Comedy*, p. 10.

30. Ter Horst, "Experienced Innocence," pp. 136–37.

31. According to John Drakakis, such alternative approaches to Shakespeare "resist, by virtue of a collective commitment to the principle of contestation of meaning, assimilation into any of the dominant traditions of Shakespeare criticism," positing instead "a series of radical transformations of the questions that can be asked of texts, a problematizing of the concept of the text itself, and a sustained critique of those critical discourses that have claimed for themselves the role of transparent mediators of the text." See Introduction, *Alternative Shakespeares*, p. 24. More specifically, Malcolm Evans offers a reassessment of Barber and Frye from a new historicist perspective in his essay "Deconstructing Shakespeare's Comedies," in Drakakis, ed., *Alternative Shakespeares*, pp. 75ff.

32. Barber, *Festive Comedy*, pp. 238–39.

# *Romeo and Juliet* as Tragicomedy: Lope's *Castelvines y Monteses* and Rojas Zorrilla's *Los bandos de Verona*

Edward H. Friedman
*Arizona State University*

ROMEO and Juliet, Shakespeare's star-crossed lovers and sacrificial offerings to social welfare, meet a happier fate in plays by two of Spain's Golden Age dramatists, Lope de Vega and Francisco de Rojas Zorrilla. This particular deviation from the source material is perhaps a question of greater interest to literary historians than to consumers of literature, given that *Castelvines y Monteses (Capulets and Montagues)* and *Los bandos de Verona (The Rival Houses of Verona)* are hardly canonical works. Nonetheless, the structure of the Spanish plays may be a statement about the *comedia* form and its public, as well as an expression of the priorities of the individual playwrights. The happy ending is, at the same time, a dramatic convention and an intertextual counterconvention; it follows Spanish Golden Age drama's resistance to tragedy in breaking with the denouement of the narratives from which it derives. Rather than renew the critical debates regarding the theory and practice of tragic drama in Habsburg Spain, this essay will examine the two plays from a structural perspective. The aim is to illuminate the choices made (and to ponder on those passed over) by the playwrights. Lope's decisions in the composition of *Castelvines y Monteses* may relate to his formula for the *comedia*, a formula which foregrounds the element of reception. Rojas Zorrilla's *Los bandos de Verona*, a tragicomic work by a writer considered to achieve tragic status in other plays, is especially interesting with respect to the dialectics of creation and appropriation.

Geoffrey Bullough, who dates *Romeo and Juliet* between 1594 and 1595, cites Masuccio Salernitano's *Il Novelino* (1476), Luigi da Porto's *Istoria novellamente ritrovata di due Nobili Amanti* (c. 1530), and Matteo Bandello's *Novelle* (1554) as Renaissance precedents which themselves have bases in Greek romance.[1] Shakespeare's play, with its emphasis on a return to harmony after the death of the protagonists, echoes the closing of da Porto's story. The Spanish plays turn away from the tragic consequences of love and the moralizing over youthful lust found in the Italian examples. The feud, the amorous attraction, the nocturnal visits, the competing suitors, the potion, and the constant threat of death remain, but the context and the dramatic aesthetic differ. Both Lope and Rojas Zorrilla prioritize love over familial honor and seem little inclined to dedicate their works to overriding social issues. Their "readings" of the sources reflect greater attention to the mechanisms of plot than to message systems. *Castelvines y Monteses* and *Los bandos de Verona* are decidedly metacritical, holding up to the public variations on a plot and revision of a tragic theme.

Lope de Vega's *Castelvines y Monteses,* dated by Morley and Bruerton between 1606 and 1612,[2] has close ties with *Romeo and Juliet* throughout the first two acts. Roselo Montes and his friend Anselmo disguise themselves as masquers to enter the home of Antonio Castelvín. At the party, Roselo falls in love with a beautiful young woman who turns out to be Julia, Don Antonio's daughter, and she is likewise enamored. When they realize that they belong to rival families, it is too late to turn back, and they marry secretly. Otavio, Julia's cousin and ardent suitor, taunts Roselo, who resists fighting with his new kinsman until he has no option other than to draw his sword. Roselo kills Otavio and is banished from Verona. Risking his life, he returns often to see Julia. Julia devises a metadramatic plot to justify her grief: she tells her father that she had married Otavio shortly before his death. Seeking a remedy, Don Antonio proposes a marriage between his daughter and the count Paris. The count, in turn, forges a letter to convince Roselo of Julia's betrayal. Julia plans to take poison rather than marry the count, but the apothecary Aurelio, in an extension of the metadrama, substitutes a soporific potion. Roselo must now prevent the premature burial of his beloved. It is at this point, scene 11 (of twenty-one) of act 3, that the play moves toward a happy ending.

Roselo rescues Julia from the tomb, and the two disguise themselves as peasants for self-protection. Meanwhile, the grief-stricken Don Antonio, seemingly bereft of heirs, plans to marry his niece Dorotea (true love of Roselo's friend Anselmo). Julia appears to the old man as a ghost and confesses that she has married Roselo and not Otavio. She convinces him not to take further vengeance on Roselo and not to marry Dorotea. When the Castelvines capture Roselo, Don Antonio pardons him. Julia abandons her ghostly stance, and the lord of Verona sanctions the marriage. Anselmo will marry Dorotea, and Roselo's faithful servant Marín wins the hand of Julia's equally faithful maid Celia. The recourses of old have been played out, but in a different mode.

The masquerade of the opening scene of *Castelvines y Monteses* sets the stage for metatheater.[3] Roselo hides his identity to commingle with the enemy faction. This is a sign of the reckless antics of which his father complains, offering as remedy a prudent marriage (scene 6). From this point forward, the enamored Roselo applies his energies (and his strategies) to overcome obstacles to his pursuit of Julia. While he cannot counteract Otavio's death wish, he defies the decree of banishment in order to visit Julia. Count Paris, suspicious of Roselo's feelings for Julia and working with Don Antonio to avenge the death, schemes to kill his opponent. The forged letter causes Roselo to doubt Julia, who has officially agreed to marry the count. The happy ending is dependent at this point on Aurelio's substitution of the potion, on communication of the plan to Roselo, and on Roselo's rescue of Julia. The successful completion of the mission averts tragedy, but the couple is still in harm's way. Julia transforms herself from peasant to ghost and elicits a crucial promise from her father, a promise that will ensure the multiple marriages at the end. In the beginning and at the conclusion of *Romeo and Juliet,* Shakespeare employs the motif of ceremony; the diversion of the masked ball cedes to the pathos of reconciliation between the surviving Montagues and Capulets. Lope balances the festivities of the opening scenes with the pledges of matrimony in the final scene. He replaces the "new society" resulting from tragedy with the comic ending (and prelude) of marriage, significantly during the harvest season. Julia's feigned death offers a key to the recourse that will save her life. As a ghostly apparition, she conquers her father's will and the stars that threaten her love. Unwilling to become victims of fate, the protagonists inscribe themselves into the metaphor of the world as stage to influence destiny and to convert tragedy into comedy. The supporting players also reap the rewards of free will. The feud ends, somewhat paradoxically, not through catharsis but through consummate dramaturgy.

Lope initiates the love plot of *Castelvines y Monteses* in the setting of the party. Roselo and his companions know that they are entering the enemy camp, but neither he nor Julia knows the identity of the love object until the infatuation is irreversible. Lope the poet recognizes the ironies of metaphor in verses which underscore the adversarial relationship. Roselo calls Julia, for example,

"Querida enemiga mía, / Luz del alma que aborreces" (My dear enemy, light of the soul that you abhor).[4] Julia's real enemy, her cousin Otavio, will not accept Roselo's offer of a truce. A captain who observes the quarrel reports to the lord of Verona that "todos dicen / Que fué de Otavio el mozo provocado / Una y mil veces, tanto que esta ofensa / Más que delito fué propia defensa" (all witnesses say that the youth was provoked by Otavio a thousand and one times, to such an extent that, rather than a crime, this was self-defense, p. 11). Since free will triumphs over determinism in the play, it is worthy of note that Lope relieves Roselo of reponsibility for the death of Otavio. It is his name rather than his actions that motivates the dramatic events; he is guilty only of loving Julia. In the name of public order, however, the lord of Verona exiles Roselo. The Castelvines swear vengeance, and Roselo falls into the trap set by Count Paris by believing that Julia has been unfaithful to him. This doubt born of pride, potentially a "tragic flaw," is short-lived. Roselo redeems himself as he sets out in search of Julia.

Awakening from the sleep induced by the drug, Julia cannot understand her condition. This time between life and death is a preparation of sorts for her appearance before her father, and the solace of the countryside gives her a chance to develop the stratagem. Lope uses the ghost not as an omen of tragedy but as an agent of plot resolution. Julia enjoys the best of both worlds. As a supernatural figure, she may make a full confession without fearing reprisal on the part of her father, who is no longer bound to the honor code. In contrast, she may exact promises from Don Antonio which will serve her in the realm of the living. Acknowledging Roselo as his son, Don Antonio ensures the happy ending. When he offers Dorotea's hand to Roselo, the flesh and blood Julia reappears to stake her prior claim, and the pairings proceed. Don Antonio's proposed marriage to Dorotea, a woman of his daughter's age, would destroy the harmony of nature; here, metadrama implies balance. The comic ending represents a restoration of peace, an end to conflict, a new beginning. Lope, in effect, synthesizes the source material with his own dramatic prescription. Adhering neither to the rules of Elizabethan tragedy nor to neoclassic re-creations of the Spanish Golden Age, *Castelvines y Monteses* exemplifies the type of play outlined in the *Arte nuevo*.

Lope respects the wishes and the passions of the young lovers, who rise above the "ancient grudge" of their families to bring forth a union of the two houses. The feud is an obstacle, a dramatic device which functions (like Don Antonio, Otavio, Count

Paris, and other characters) to complicate the action and to prolong the denouement. Roselo stands far above the rival suitors, one of whom is self-destructive, the other malicious. Moreover, his love is reciprocated. His actions are rational and directed by love. He puts himself in danger to maintain ties with Julia and to avert further tragedy. Don Antonio, whose allegiance to honor is understandable, jeopardizes that very honor in his betrothal to Dorotea. Julia's "death" for love would be desecrated by this marriage. The poison that would write Julia out of the plot is, mercifully, recast as a soporific. The misinterpretation on Roselo's part that would have had him believe that Julia was dead is countered by her awakening before his arrival at the vault. Similarly, Roselo's capture by Teobaldo, Otavio's father, takes place after the "spirit" Julia wins a pardon. Both Count Paris and Teobaldo accept the decision as divinely inspired, and the return of the real Julia is the final marker of tragedy superseded.

The unity of action of *Castelvines y Monteses* is based on the movement toward a sanctioned union of Roselo and Julia, that is, on the linking of love and honor, on the progression from separation to consolidation. The party setting of the opening scenes serves as an escape from the civil turmoil. Roselo and Julia are nameless, and thus free of the binds of identity, free to love. The dramatic events are, in essence, a search for society's blessing of the love. The honor-bound fathers, the persistent suitors, the defenders of each house, and the administrators of social justice block the spiritual victory, if not the marriage, of the protagonists. (As is typical in the *comedia*, the figure of the mother, who would presumably supply a dose of sympathy, is absent.) The longer the lovers are separated, the graver the threat to their well-being. Julia would rather die than face marriage to Count Paris, yet Roselo allows himself to doubt her devotion. Time and chance are on their side, and once they are reunited, they have greater control over their fate. They adopt new identities, bucolic and phantasmic, to win the struggle of love over the body politic.

Donald R. Wadley distinguishes between Shakespeare's favoring of parental authority over the freedom of choice and Lope's unabashed sympathy for the plight of the protagonists. He sees a tension in *Romeo and Juliet* between the refusal of the two families to cease their feud, as ordered by the Prince of Verona, and their demand for absolute obedience on the part of the young lovers. Emphasis on retribution makes punishment inevitable, even though the extent of the punishment, according to Wadley, most certainly surpasses the crime.[5] That disequilibrium may be the essence of tragedy. Shakespeare's play projects a conflict of the heart against the head—freedom of choice versus respect for authority—while Lope's play answers in favor of the individual will. In *Castelvines y Monteses,* Lope reduces the impact of the feud by relegating the question of authority to a lesser plane. In this way, he circumvents what Wadley would consider an irony of Shakespeare's version: that what causes the heads of the families to act sensibly is not the prince's demand for a truce but the death of their children. The Spanish play settles the dispute without the sacrifice and without unduly compromising the authority figures. The lesson conveyed is consonant with individual rights and with the collective good, and it emanates from the protagonists themselves, who master theatrical recourses (and the intertext) to become masters of their fate.

Bandello's story admonishes youth to govern their desires and to control their passions. *Romeo and Juliet* focuses, as well, on the chain of command within families and within society at large. It would be wrong, of course, to consider the play in a purely doctrinaire context. Shakespeare's art is consciously poetic and consciously tragic, and the ritualistic sacrifice lends itself to both levels of creation. *Castelvines y Monteses* illustrates Lope's break from the dictates of the past. His rules of decorum accept the blending of comedy and tragedy and the juxtaposition of various forms of verse. Always directed toward the popular audience, the *vulgo,* the plays may reflect a greater preoccupation with attention span than with abstraction. There is a tendency in plays such as *Fuenteovejuna* to highlight individual freedom without disrupting the hierarchical order of the State.[6] In the ideological sense, *Castelvines y Monteses* is hardly revolutionary. The play opposes civil strife, arguably as staunchly as it defends a woman's prerogative to choose her mate. As representative of the State, the lord of Verona is eminently just. He exiles Roselo, who has acted in self-defense, as much to protect him as to prevent further violence. Roselo and Julia seem admirably suited for each other, despite the omission of their families from the selection process. Don Antonio's proposal of marriage to Dorotea is far less suitable, despite the wisdom of his years. (Even the peasants question his judgment.) Julia's taste of death gives her final ploy added credibility and thematic weight. In the last scene, Roselo and Julia regain the identities lost from the moment of their attraction. Society will now let them portray themselves.

Lope fits the source material into the *comedia* framework, of which he is the principal designer and proponent. The shift from tragedy to tragicomedy is a radical modification if one sees the story as an indictment against youthful lust, but less so if one accentuates the restoration of order. Shakespeare's Romeo and Juliet are pawns in the cleansing process, and their roles seem to relate more to catharsis than to morality. The chorus in the prologue and the father in the closing scene bear witness to the sacrificial nature of the play. Lope effects change without a purge; the constant threats to Roselo's safety and the figurative death of Julia are sufficient to "bury their parents' strife." The playwright does not force the plot line into the tragicomic mold, as does Guillén de Castro, to cite one example, in *Progne y Filomena* (c. 1610). In this story, whose earliest source is Ovid's *Metamorphoses,* a young boy is the sacrificial victim, the object of vengeance for his father's crime. Castro ends act 2 at this point, allows seventeen years to pass, and introduces two new protagonists to bring about a happy ending in act 3.[7] The lack of verisimilitude in Castro's play underscores the smooth transitions of *Castelvines y Monteses.*

The critical studies of A. A. Parker present the thesis that tragedy, Aristotelian or Elizabethan, is generally incompatible with the worldview of seventeenth-century Spain. Parker regards poetic justice as the common denominator of Golden Age drama. Characters are responsible, accountable, for their actions; there is no place in this system for the innocent victims of tragedy.[8] It is possible that Lope's concept of tragicomedy does not rely as heavily as Parker would have it on poetic justice as a moral criterion. Justice, as served by the *comedia,* must be defined in specific (that is, relative) terms and, in most cases, from a single perspective. The Calderonian honor plays, for example, are not lacking in victims, nor is their brand of justice unambiguous. *Admiratio,* in the form of spectacular death scenes, is not absent from the theater of the Golden Age. In the *Arte nuevo,* Lope advocates tragicomedy because variety pleases the public ("aquesta variedad deleita mucho"), which may make his motives pragmatic rather than moral or intellectual. What is obvious in *Castelvines y Monteses* is his ability to adapt tragedy to his model for the *comedia.* It is not a given, however, that the spirit of the times demands this change. As Raymond R. MacCurdy points out, the third Spanish play on the topic, Cristóbal de Rozas's *Los amantes de Verona* (1666), maintains the tragic ending of the Italian novelle.[9] While the middle play, Rojas Zorrilla's *Los bandos de Verona* (1640) follows Lope's happy ending, critics such as MacCurdy classify a number of Rojas Zorrilla's works as tragedies.

Rojas Zorrilla was a favorite of King Felipe IV, who commissioned him to write a play for the opening of the coliseum theater in the Buen Retiro palace in Madrid. For this royal occasion, Rojas Zorrilla composed *Los bandos de Verona,* which was staged by Cosme Lotti, an Italian "master of elaborate apparatus and sensational stage machinery."[10] Although the audience and the theater stand in contrast to Lope's public and the *corrales,* or courtyard theaters, the direction of the play is similar to that of *Castelvines y Monteses.* The major difference may lie in the playwrights' control of the material and in the internal logic of the works. Rojas Zorrilla arrives at a happy ending by way of a dramatic structure that reveals a Baroque sensibility wrought, in part, by the mediating presence of Calderón. *Los bandos de Verona* is rich in words and devices, and its artifice is not dependent solely on the tricks of Lotti's trade. The fact that Rojas Zorrilla ventured into tragedy on other occasions makes his tragicomedy of Romeo and Juliet a document of special interest, a text which bears traces of tradition and signs of creative freedom.

Lope's *Castelvines y Monteses* opens with Roselo's entry into Don Antonio's home. In the dialogue with his cousin Anselmo, he provides the play's exposition without delaying the action. By scene 4, he has met and fallen in love with Julia and she with him. In the first scene of *Los bandos de Verona,*[12] Julia Capelete commiserates with Elena Romeo, sister of Alejandro Romeo and wife of Count Paris. Rojas Zorrilla creates a parallel discourse in which Julia complains of an impossible love (for her family's enemy Alejandro) and Elena of unbearable disdain (on the part of her husband). In a speech of 264 verses, Julia explains the causes of the enmity, her first encounter with Alejandro, the ensuing courtship, and the desire of her cousin Andrés to marry her. The two women are linked not only by the ties to Alejandro but by the Count's plan to have his marriage annulled in order to wed Julia. Preferring death to his current suffering, Alejandro enters the house to confront Julia's father, Don Antonio. She dissuades him, and they arrange a meeting for that night. The death imagery of the lovers' speeches acknowledges the tragic source, as well as poetic convention. While hiding, Alejandro overhears the requests of Andrés and Count Paris for the hand of Julia, and the plans of the count and Don Antonio to do battle against the Montescos, with Alejandro himself as their first target. Julia confesses her love for Alejandro ("mi esposo y dueño" [husband and master]), thereby incurring the wrath of her father and the jealousy of her suitors. Alejandro and his cousin Carlos defend themselves against their adversaries, and only Elena's pleas prevent her brother from killing the count. Act 1 ends with the protagonists begging the heavens to bring them together.

The addition of Elena Romeo to the dramatis personae allows Rojas Zorrilla to sustain a discursive symmetry while emphasizing the antithetical situations of the two women, both victims of the family rivalry. Elena's intervention in the final scene of the first act keeps Count Paris, an admirably nefarious antagonist, alive. One cannot help but wonder, however, what motivated the count to marry her and why she, born a Montesco, is welcome among the Castelvines, or why the dramatist is willing to concede her "pathetic" space equal to Julia's. Another major figure of *Los bandos de Verona* is Guardainfante, Alejandro's servant and the play's *gracioso*. In *Castelvines y Monteses,* Roselo's servant Marín and the peasants provide comic relief, the former through his fear of entering the funeral vault and the latter in their commentary on the theme of matrimony. Rojas Zorrilla expands the role of the servant to put him in burlesque confrontations with the enemy. (Two of his speeches in act 1 are second in length only to Julia's expository speech.) In his first entrance on stage, Guardainfante is covered with plaster, and his ghostlike demeanor foreshadows the sequence of Julia's "death" in the second half of the play.

Act 2 produces further complications. Setting a time and a place for the rendezvous, Alejandro sends a note to Julia via Guardainfante, who continues to deliver bits of humor. The servant gives the note to Elena, who believes that she is the intended recipient. In the meantime, Don Antonio gives Julia an ultimatum: she must marry either Andrés or Count Paris. Julia will not forsake Alejandro, and her father, infuriated, threatens to kill her. He orders her to choose between death by the sword or by poison. In desperation, she reiterates her love for Alejandro and drinks the vial of poison. The distraught Don Antonio declares that he only wished to intimidate her. When he hears of the incident from Guardainfante, Alejandro heads to the church (where he had planned to meet Julia) to see whether the report is true. Elsewhere, Andrés explains to his servant that when Don Antonio asked him to obtain a poison, ostensibly for a traitorous maid, he substituted a mixture of opium and henbane, believing (correctly) that Julia was the object of her father's wrath. Since he knows that she is alive, he proceeds to the church. The final scenes of act 2 are a testament to the extremes of tragicomedy. Don Antonio, the count, and Andrés align to pursue Alejandro. Alejandro discovers Julia with the dubious aid of Guardainfante, whose fear exceeds that of Marín in *Castelvines y Monteses*. The grief of the one and the apprehensiveness of the other are mitigated by Julia's awakening. In the darkness, Alejandro attempts to escape with Julia but attaches himself to Elena by mistake, while Julia, in turn, is carried off by Andrés.

Following Lope's advice in the *Arte nuevo,* Rojas Zorrilla employs a common set of recourses for the numerous crises of act 2. Guardainfante does not make clear to Elena the intention of the letter. Don Antonio goes too far in defending his honor and Alejandro not far enough in protecting Julia. An opiate takes the place of poison, and the sleep it induces poses as death. As at the end of act 1, Elena (here, unwittingly) intensifies the conflict and prolongs the agony of the lovers. Guardainfante's cowardice in the church cemetery provides more than comic relief; it detracts from Alejandro's lament over the "death" of Julia. Perhaps the greatest intrusion in the second act is Andrés's sixty-line explanation of the drug substitution, a plot device which seems unnecessarily farfetched. This particular alteration of the source material may not be for the better.

In act 3, Don Antonio continues his search for Alejandro but instead finds Julia, whom he takes to be a ghost. Unlike her counterpart in *Castelvines y Montesses,* Julia derives no benefit from the illusion. Supported by the two scorned suitors, Don Antonio imprisons her (along with Elena and Carlos) in a castle and announces to the enemy camp that she is dead. To avenge the alleged crime, Alejandro lays siege to the castle and refuses to yield to the pleas of those trapped inside, including his sister and his cousin. Finally, Don Antonio brings out Julia to beg for mercy, and the grateful lover calls off the attack, on the condition that he be allowed to marry Julia and that Elena be reconciled with Count Paris. The closing speech, which contains an allusion to the new theater, signals as well the "dichoso fin" of the play.

Darkness, disguise, and confusion lead to the catastrophic ending of act 2 of *Los bandos de Verona.* Julia, given a second life by the potion, finds herself at the mercy of an embittered Andrés, who attempts to violate her. She escapes, only to fall into the hands of the count and her father. (Rojas Zorrilla transmits this information, in a somewhat jocular manner, through a speech of 106 lines delivered by Guardainfante.) Julia has little success at metatheatrics; her appearance as a ghost wins no concessions from her father, and she is unable to flee. She remains in the castle with the Castelvín loyalists and other prisoners. The final decisive action belongs to Alejandro, who believes until the very end that Julia is dead. In a moment of high suspense, Rojas Zorrilla chooses to relegate the unparalleled love of Alejandro for Julia to his demand for vengeance. Neither his sister nor the cousin who has saved his life can convince Alejandro to change his mind. When Julia is once more brought to life, it is not surprising that he orders a halt to the siege. The play's resolution is more a matter of force than a rational end to the feud, but one can assume that love will conquer all, if Don Antonio and Count Paris are men of their word.

The possibility of tragedy exists throughout the third act. Julia's father and her suitors could kill her to save their honor and their pride. Or, in a supreme stroke of irony, she could die in the siege of the castle through a misdirected act of revenge. Unmoved by Elena and Carlos, Alejandro could destroy the object of his love. While the threat of tragedy is a cornerstone of tragicomedy, the rigor of Alejandro's mission may lower him in the spectator's estimation. The fact that he will sacrifice (innocent) members of his family to make a point compromises the denouement, intrudes, as it were, on the scales of justice. As a corollary, Don Antonio, when put to the test, embraces life over honor; he is not prepared to die so that his honor may live. He uses Julia as a shield, and he accedes to Alejandro's demands. Whereas Lope manages to effect a catharsis without tragedy in *Castelvines y Monteses,* Rojas Zorrilla effects a surrender. Don Antonio agrees to be Alejandro's father, the count his friend. Carlos forgives him, and the play is over.

In his analysis of *Romeo and Juliet,* Wadley suggests that the loss of life is a lamentable price to pay for a truce already mandated by the Prince of Verona: "the pity of it is that two innocent lives had to be destroyed in order to bring a pair of irascible old men to their senses."[12] There is a clear lack of nobility in the intransigence of Montague and Capulet, but that, one might argue, only strengthens the tragic import of the play. There is no need for the protagonists to die. In *Castelvines y Monteses,* Lope avoids the problem of a disproportion between crime and punishment by preserving life and honor. The intertextual scenario casts the lovers into tragedy. Lope as dramatist and his characters as metadramatists impose themselves, or impose comedy, on the tragic script. They rewrite the death scene as a simulacrum of death in accordance with the conventions of the cloak and sword play, the *comedia de capa y espada.* For Lope, the message seems to have less to do with authority than with the course of true love. Lest one criticize the treatment of Don Antonio as authority figure, Lope makes his choice of bridegrooms (Otavio and Count Paris) singularly unattractive and his decision to wed Dorotea the object of mockery. Roselo and Julia are benevolent warriors against convention, social and dramatic.

Like Lope's play, *Los bandos de Verona* redirects the tragic plot. Rojas Zorrilla seems intent upon retaining the devices of the source material while incorporating new characters and situations. The result is a concept of tragicomedy in which comedy *intrudes* upon (to repeat a term used earlier) the serious business of the stage. The *gracioso* Guardainfante supplies comic diversion at the expense of tone, or consistency of mood. His description of Julia's near-rape by Andrés, for example, belies the gravity of the circumstance. This is not comic restatement or variation of the theme, but, in certain instances, an inversion of priorities. Lope adapts the potion and the ghostly appearance of Julia to his re-created plot, while Rojas Zorrilla begs the question of plausibility in the case of the potion and negates the validity of the ghost motif. Given the shift from love to vengeance, the climactic episode of the siege in *Los bandos de Verona* would probably have more force as tragedy than as (tragi)comedy. While other versions of the story stress differences between the protagonists and their elders, Rojas Zorrilla's depiction of Alejandro at the end of act 3 shows that the experience may have taught the hero only that history is destined to repeat itself. He apparently has not learned that life is precious and of greater value than honor. If he cannot have Julia, he will sacrifice his sister and cousin in the name of revenge. Expressed in more comprehensive terms, the brush with tragedy does not have the same impact in *Los bandos de Verona* that it has in *Castelvines y Monteses*. The retelling distorts the focus, and tragicomedy leads not to delightful variation but to mixed messages.

If Lope demonstrates how a tragic plot can be redesigned to accommodate his formula for the *comedia,* Rojas Zorrilla's dramatic (re)vision is more difficult to classify. MacCurdy makes the following observation: "Many Spanish dramatists, even when treating material essentially tragic, often contrived a happy ending. Rojas was of a different mold. Although he did not entirely escape the dramatic conventions of his day, saving the skins of his Romeo and Juliet in *Los bandos de Verona,* he was prone to permit a pattern of incidents directed toward catastrophe to pursue the natural course, or even to fabricate a fortuitous turn of events to provide an unhappy ending."[13] An example is the play based on Cervantes's *Persiles y Sigismunda,* in which the playwright changes the traditional ending of romance to have the protagonists die in a fall from a castle wall. MacCurdy's study of Rojas Zorrilla's works leads him to the conclusion that "Rojas' tragic art represents a return to Spanish tragedy as it was cultivated a half-century earlier—before Lope de Vega forged the new, all-purposeful *comedia*. There are in Rojas' tragedies, as in those of Juan de la Cueva and his followers, the same concern with the Senecan themes of revenge and fortune, the same preoccupation with exaggerated tragic types, the same cult of violence, the same unrestrained expression of emotion."[14] One of the tragedies is *Progne y Filomena* (1636), which in Guillén de Castro's version acquires a happy ending. At the end of Rojas Zorrilla's play, in a manifestation of unrestrained passion, the two sisters fight over who has the right to take revenge on the adulterous husband of one and the violater of the other. "As it turns out, the sisters compromise, joining together to riddle Tereo's body. The audience is then treated to a view of the corpse in the blood-spattered bed."[15]

How does one explain the structure of *Los bandos de Verona* in light of the judgment that Rojas Zorrilla's tragedies comprise the only real body of *tragedias patéticas*, in the phrase of El Pinciano, in seventeenth-century Spain?[16] Even MacCurdy, one of the dramatist's strongest advocates, calls the play "outrageous."[17] The success of Lope's *comedia* and the existence of *Castelvines y Monteses*, together with the decline of tragedy, may provide a partial answer, but Rojas Zorrilla's frequent recourse to the tragic mode indicates a willingness to explore new (or old) territory. Another explanation, also less than definitive, is that the source material does not follow the particular form of tragedy, primarily Senecan in orientation, imitated by Rojas Zorrilla. The final scenes of *Los bandos de Verona* leave open the option of impassioned grief and bloodshed. Alejandro could avenge Julia's "death," only to find that his aggression was the cause of her real death; one can imagine lofty speeches in which he orders the death of those in the castle, recognizes that he has inadvertently murdered his beloved, and contemplates suicide (a logical conclusion under these circumstances). This is the road not taken by Rojas Zorrilla, and one can merely speculate on the choices made.

My feeling (or "reading") is that Rojas Zorrilla assumed that his public had at least a general knowledge of the source story, whether through Lope's play, with its happy ending, or not. The interplay of familiarity, expectation, and innovation, coupled with the numerous versions of the story, could result in the lack of clarity and emotional crosscurrents of *Los bandos de Verona;* perhaps the dramatist did not have a fixed direction when composing the work. As a final stage of second guessing, I would submit that the dramatic structure, and especially the comic ending, may have been precipitated by the auspicious occasion for which it was commissioned. The opening of the theater and the debut performance before the king and courtiers may have had something to do with the decision not to sacrifice the young lovers. The Baroque idiom of the play combines the lyric complexity of the protagonists' discourse with the puns and "cultured" popular style of the *gracioso*,[18] and it seems likely that Rojas Zorrilla wrote the play with an eye on spectacle and on the talents of Cosme Lotti.

In *New Readings vs. Old Plays*, Richard Levin categorizes much of recent literary criticism as ironic commentary aimed at the vindication of minor works or authors (and, not unrelatedly, at the elevation of the critic). He cautions, "All of these readings, we must remember, maintain that they have left the play a better work of art than they found it—indeed, this is said to be the purpose of each reading and its justification."[19] The present study of structure in *Castelvines y Montentes* and *Los bandos de Verona* has a different focus, perhaps equally ironic. This approach sees value in placing texts against each other, finding enrichment in the process of selection and in the notion of intertextuality. *Romeo and Juliet* has a place in Spanish Golden Age drama. The works by Lope de Vega and Francisco de Rojas Zorrilla, if not "alike in dignity," are signs of their times and, ultimately, stories about playwriting.

## Notes

1. Geoffrey Bullough, ed., *Narrative and Dramatic Sources of Shakespeare* (New York: Columbia University Press, 1957), 1:269–72.
2. S. Griswold Morley and Courtney Bruerton, *The Chronology of Lope de Vega's Comedias* (New York: The Modern Language Association of America, 1940), p. 182.
3. See Lionel Abel, *Metatheatre: A New View of Dramatic Form* (New York: Hill and Wang, 1963).
4. Lope de Vega, *Comedias escogidas de Frey Lope Félix de Vega Carpio*, Biblioteca de Autores Españoles, 52 (Madrid: Ediciones Atlas, 1952), 4:7. Subsequent quotations from *Castelvines y Montentes* will refer to this edition. Page numbers will be indicated in parentheses. See Lope de Vega, *El arte nuevo de hacer comedias en este tiempo*, ed. Juana de José Prades (Madrid: Consejo Superior de Investigaciones Científicas, 1971).
5. Donald R. Wadley, "Lope and Shakespeare," *The American Hispanist* 4 (1979): 19.
6. On this topic, see, for example, Donald R. Larson, *The Honor Plays of Lope de Vega* (Cambridge: Harvard University Press, 1977), and Frank P. Casa, "Affirmation and Retraction in Golden Age Drama," *Neophilologus* 61 (1977): 551–64. See also Walter Cohen, *Drama of a Nation: Public Theater in Renaissance England and Spain* (Ithaca: Cornell University Press, 1985).
7. For the text of *Progne y Filomena*, see Guillén de Castro, *Obras de Don Guillén de Castro*

*y Bellvis,* ed. Eduardo Juliá Martínez, vol. 1 (Madrid: Tipografía de la "Revista de Archivos," 1925).

8. See, for example, A. A. Parker, *The Approach to the Spanish Drama of the Golden Age* (London: The Hispanic and Luso-Brazilian Councils, 1957), and "Towards a Definition of Calderonian Tragedy," *Bulletin of Hispanic Studies* 39 (1962): 222–37.

9. Raymond R. MacCurdy, *Francisco de Rojas Zorrilla* (New York: Twayne, 1968), p. 108.

10. Francis C. Hayes, *Lope de Vega* (New York: Twayne, 1967), p. 57.

11. For the text, see Francisco de Rojas Zorrilla, *Comedias escogidas de Rojas Zorrilla,* Biblioteca de Autores Españoles, 54 (Madrid: Ediciones Atlas, 1952), pp. 367–88.

12. Wadley, "Lope and Shakespeare," p. 19.

13. Raymond R. MacCurdy, *Francisco de Rojas Zorrilla and the Tragedy* (Albuquerque: University of New Mexico Press, 1958), p. 24.

14. Ibid., p. 139.

15. MacCurdy, *Francisco de Rojas Zorrilla,* p. 51. See Enrique Martínez Vidal, "Katharsis and Comic Relief in Rojas Zorrilla's *Progne y Filomena,*" in *Josep Maria Solà-Solé: Homage, homenaje, homenatge,* ed. Antonio Torres-Alcalá et al. (Barcelona: Puvill, 1984), 2: 85–90; and Dietrich Briesemeister, "El horror y su función en algunas tragedias de Francisco de Rojas Zorrilla," *Criticón* 23 (1983): 159–75.

16. MacCurdy, *Rojas Zorrilla and the Tragedy,* p. 139.

17. MacCurdy, *Francisco de Rojas Zorrilla,* p. 108.

18. The lyric beauty of the play seems especially evident in Alejandro's apostrophe to night (p. 375), Julia's plea to her father for freedom of choice in marriage (p. 377), Alejandro's reaction to the news of Julia's death (p. 379), and his discovery that she is alive (p. 381). The page numbers refer to the Biblioteca de Autores Españoles edition.

19. Richard Levin, *New Readings vs. Old Plays* (Chicago: University of Chicago Press, 1979), p. 129.

# *Hamlet* and *El médico de su honra:* The Significance of Intrigue

Bruce Golden

*California State University, San Bernardino*

SOME 1590 lines into the play, Shakespeare's Hamlet finds himself trapped agonizingly in frustrating passivity. He has sworn vengeance on his father's murderer but has so far been unable to act against him. This is understandable because his adversary is not only his own uncle, but, by virtue of having recently married his mother, Claudius is also King of Denmark. Even so, these plausible excuses only exacerbate his frustration. Prompted by the visiting player's speech, Hamlet launches into a tirade—the "O what a rogue and peasant slave am I!" soliloquy—in the course of which he berates himself for his inaction:

>                 This is most brave,
> That I, the son of a dear father murder'd,
> Prompted to my revenge by heaven and hell,
> Must like a whore unpack my heart with words
> And fall a-cursing like a very drab,
> A scullion! Fie upon't! Foh![1]
>
> [2.2.578–83]

Lacking deeds, words have become his only weapons, but they are aimed at himself, full only of sound and fury. Indeed, they add to his mounting frustration.

In *El médico de su honra*, Don Gutierre echoes Hamlet almost at the same point in the developing action—about 1580 lines into Calderón's tragedy.[2] He laments because he also is unable to act in accordance with his desires and thus is deeply frustrated:

> ¿Podré ya quejarme? Sí;
> pero consolarme, no.
> Ya estoy solo, ya bien puedo .
> hablar. ¡Ay Dios! Quién supiera
> reducir solo a un discurso,
> medir con sola una idea
> tantos géneros de agravios,
> tantos linajes de penas

                como cobardes me asaltan,
                como atrevidos me cercan!

                [2. 567–76]

                Have I cause to complain?
                Yes, but not for consolation.
                Now that I am alone, I
                am free to speak. O God! if I
                could reduce to only one discourse, to
                measure with only one idea all sorts of
                insults, all lineages of sorrows that
                assault me cowardly, that encircle me boldly.

In Calderón's tragedy, Don Gutierre's adversary also has royal blood: his antagonist is the king's brother. So he, too, finds consolation only in speech at this juncture. Neither can act otherwise to further his cause. This phenomenon of two heroes, committed to vengeance, responding similarly at a near-identical point during the *protasis* of a seventeenth-century tragedy might not be that surprising, but it is worth consideration. After all, if this similarity exists, other resemblances between Shakespeare's tragedy and Calderón's *comedia* may exist; these should be worth observing in two such different national literatures at the height of their achievement in drama.

Drama in Renaissance England and Spain (roughly between 1580–1640) has generally been studied, John Loftis reminds us, to determine which English dramatists read Spanish and therefore (supposedly) used *Siglo de Oro* drama for sources.[3] However, other approaches prove useful. Historians and critics of the period have begun to redefine their focus to include, even make fundamental to their approach, "a series of correlations and causations among economic and social structures, political systems, cultural milieus [and] theatrical institutions."[4] These approaches share the recognition that Spain and England—enemies in religion and rivals in imperial ambition—developed simultaneously a popular (as opposed to a courtly or aristocratic) theater. But the divergent methodologies the approaches require cannot readily be harmonized, and the dramas themselves are often obscured by the larger political issues for which they serve as evidence.

Another means of comparison is available. Instead of examining sources—alleged or assumed—for the dramatic traditions, and instead of using those traditions as the basis for a more sweeping cultural comparison, I propose a modest study in comparative dramaturgy. My focus, then, is not on the ideological basis of the nascent absolutist state, but on the way two particular plays—Shakespeare's *Hamlet* and Calderón's *El médico de su honra*—use certain cultural assumptions dramatically to further their plotting and characterization. For my purpose it is beside the point if Calderón is endorsing or criticizing the code of honor, or Shakespeare the code of revenge: what matters is how these two playwrights exploit these conventions in their plays.

From one perspective:

> In drama, character depends on function: what a character is follows from what he has to do in the play. Dramatic function in turn depends on the structure of the play; the character has certain things to do because the play has such and such a shape.[5]

This kind of approach reveals a number of consistencies in characterization that transcend historical determinants in favor of generic factors. It throws into relief matters of plot as well, taking us back to the examples cited at the beginning of this essay. At that point both Hamlet and Don Gutierre find themselves deeply imbedded in an action that almost overdetermines their activities. As Shakespeare and Calderón plot their tragedies, the hero does not choose to be where he finds himself. Hamlet, in a sense, has had his father's ghost thrust upon him, and Don Gutierre finds himself passively implicated in the action at the very opening of the play: Prince Enrique falls accidentally from a horse and is carried into Don Gutierre's home, where Doña Mencía, Don Gutierre's wife, encounters her former love. Both know immediately the possible ramifications for themselves and for each other, but they are as helpless as her husband to work themselves out of what becomes the tragic bind caused by the stipulations of an unrelenting honor code to which they all subscribe.

Prince Enrique impetuously, but foolishly, visits Doña Mencía at night, dropping his dagger and leaving it behind. Her husband discovers it, and after eavesdropping on a conversation between the Prince and his brother, King Don Pedro, in a 132-line soliloquy (some of which is quoted above) he proclaims his allegiance to the honor code which, if adhered to, will bring about his wife's death. Don Gutierre is not responsible for his own honor being called into question by his wife's visitor. But he ultimately reduces interpretations of events to astonishing simplicity:

> Y así acortemos discursos,
> pues todos juntos se cierran
> en que Mencía es quien es,
> y yo soy quien soy;

> And thus we cut short our discourse,
> Since all arguments conclude that she
> is Mencía, and I am who I am;

He continues, at first attempting to deny any fault:

> No hay quien pueda
> borrar de tanto esplendor
> la hermosura y la pureza.
>
> No one alive can cast a slur upon
> her bright effulgence of so much
> beauty and such purity.

But he quickly reverses himself:

> Pero sí puede, mal digo;
> que al Sol una nube negra,
> si no le mancha, le turba,
> si no le eclipsa, le hiela.
>
> I speak wrongly, for a black
> cloud can dim the sun.

He then questions the damning code while at the same time invoking it:

> ¿Qué injusta ley condena,
> que muera el inocente y que padezca?
> A peligro estáis, honor,
> no hay hora en vos que no sea
> crítica, en vuestro sepulcro
> vivís, puesto que os alienta
> la mujer, en ella estáis
> pisando siempre la huesa.
> Y os he de curar, honor.
> [2.631–49]
>
> What unjust decree is this whereby the
> innocent are doomed to suffer death? You
> are in peril honor. Each hour you live
> is so critical that you are already
> living in your tomb, because a woman
> guards your life. In woman your
> safety lives—and walks on skulls and
> bones. I shall have to cure you honor.

Don Gutierre automatically makes that desperate, argumentative leap that irrevocably determines his character, exerting a fatal influence on his actions. He keeps working out quite logical conclusions from absurd premises, then feels himself bound by that logic rather than by any real, human desire.

By Calderón's time, for at least five hundred years women had been made responsible for preserving a man's honor. By the twelfth century the old Roman concept of *probitas* (a valor of both body and soul that produced both prowess and magnanimity . . . transmitted through the blood)[6] had become central to the aristocratic code of values. The belief that the blood of both husband and wife contributed to the character of an offspring gave men the reason to concern themselves with their wife's fidelity. Their own, of course, did not matter, because what was at stake was nothing so abstract or basic as virtue, as we understand it, but only the character of any legitimate male offspring. The male heir had to bear an honorable name and carry especially honorable blood. It was the woman alone, then, who would be responsible for any impurity in the blood line, for only her infamy could introduce an impure strain into the family. While this general concept was the basis for any aristocratic code of values in medieval Europe, in Spain the purity of blood issue swelled in importance against the background of seven-hundred years of Moorish presence and Jewish influence. By Calderón's day, concern over family honor and purity of blood had reached nearly hysterical proportions. Controversy seethed publicly and privately over the status of anyone with Moorish or Jewish bloodlines. Christian Spaniards insisted upon their superiority and naturally "pure" blood and honor. This kind of personal honor gave the male Spaniard a sense of "being" that established him as a virile, prudent guardian of his family and his name. Yet finally, Don Gutierre's behavior reveals that his appeal to honor only mystifies his urge to subjugate his wife.[7]

In his role as protector, Don Gutierre acts outrageously. Yet he has rationalized that outrage in advance. As soon as he casts himself in the role of acting as physician of his own honor, all that remains is to follow the code he had so thoroughly criticized as irrational in the speech cited above. He embarks upon the course that will indeed preserve his own sense of honor, but at a gruesomely tragic price. In Shakespeare's revenge tragedy, Hamlet also unhesitatingly binds himself to a role dictated to him. In this case, it is his father's command:

*Ham.* Speak, I am bound to hear.
*Gho.* So art thou to revenge when thou shalt hear.
. . . . . . . . . . . . . .

> *Ham.* I'll wipe away all trivial fond records,
> All saws of books, all forms, all pressures past
> That youth and observation copied there,
> And thy commandment all alone shall live
> Within the book and volume of my brain,
> Unmix'd with baser matter.
>
> [1.5.7–8, 99–104]

For Hamlet, too, this is hardly a matter of choice. What dutiful son could not swear to avenge a murdered father—especially against Claudius, for whom Hamlet had already expressed undisguised contempt (in 1.2.65ff.)? Shakespeare makes no issue of Hamlet's oath; his problems develop as the stipulations of the oath beg to be met. Likewise, everyone accepts the conditions of the honor code in Calderón's world, and the tragedy develops as the code's stipulations become manifest in the play's action.

Interestingly, both codes of behavior (that of honor in Spain, revenge in England) determine in large measure the choices made by each hero as he pursues his tragic quest. As such, they reveal fundamental aspects of each hero's character. As the heroes respond to the mounting pressures exerted by events which are often out of their control, they come to seem almost trapped in the conventions which govern their behavior. Each realizes slowly what it means to adhere to a code which each recognizes at the same time as binding, barbaric, and inflexible. Baldly stated, these codes demand that the heroes suffer their predicament in silence, live their lives in considerable isolation and secrecy, indulge in sometimes extravagantly crafty but always prudent intrigues in response to their circumstances, eventually recognize the proper occasion to strike openly, finally bringing about a murderous, bloody catastrophe by which the hero maintains his own honor, or—in the case of the revenge ethic—he achieves vengeance at the cost of his own life. Dramaturgically, these elements become *topoi* of a tragic plot. They describe the heroes' behavior of suffering, silence, and dissimulation while awaiting the occasion to bring about the tragic catastrophe.[8] These heroes behave this way because they believe that only by carrying out the tenets of the honor or revenge code can they continue to function. Everything done while following these precepts is explained in their dialogue, like copy-book maxims found in dozens of authorized texts. Indeed, as maxims or aphorisms they appear in approved, educational texts to exemplify as well as justify patterns of behavior to educated people in the Renaissance. Looked at characterologically, the maxims serve fundamentally as rationalizations to help explain the heroes' extreme actions as they struggle to regain control over their own lives. Finally, we can see that these texts which dictate manners and morals of Renaissance life include advice to justify even the most reprehensible acts.

The prudent duplicity and secrecy that occur while delaying vengeance, the silent suffering, the deeply felt obligation extending even to murder in order to restore honor and accomplish revenge all contribute to a deliberate pattern. These activities that drive forward the plot are engrafted onto a societal ethic that defines and encompasses basic human endeavor, but they produce ambivalent and contradictory responses in both on-stage characters and audience. Most of us have felt the urge to avenge ourselves for crimes or injustices perpetrated against us, or have felt the necessity to fight in order to preserve our own honor when we fear being shamed. Yet we also normally recognize how empty revenge can be. It succeeds only temporarily in rescuing the ego from its embarrassment. For the male, moreover, the honor code establishes the discomforting premise that in any family a woman's shame brings about a male's dishonor. Masculine honor, then, can be seen as an ego defense that produces acceptable, even approved, social strategies which shape one's behavior but which serve primarily to disguise feelings of unconscious rage focused mostly on women. When this rage explodes, irrational responses threaten to overcome the ego's rational power. In turn, the ego's reflex in reasserting itself will go to extreme lengths to regain its control of character, and, in this state of mind, all sorts of actions begin to be seen as necessary parts of an honor or revenge code. The suspicion, secrecy, dissimulating, eavesdropping, lying, all eventually leading to murder, become part of the ego's activity to reestablish authority and control over the unconscious.

Hamlet's depression has begun before the play begins. It seems to be centered in his mother's hasty remarriage ("Frailty, thy name is woman," 1.2.146), but the focus changes after his conversation with his father's ghost. On the other hand, Calderón's tragedy focuses on honor, an ever-present anxiety for a *Siglo de Oro* audience. Don Gutierre, caught up in his own preoccupations, acts in accordance with the manuals' advice, as does Hamlet, the hero following the revenge code. Each is driven to tragic extremes as he attempts to master, through rationalized means of ego-controlled behavior, his irrational anger.

Prudence turns out to be the crucial value for both heroes. The first mark of prudent behavior will be their discreet silence, attempting to keep the insult to their own honor as secret as possible. Aphorisms emphasizing the virtue of silence abound in sixteenth- and seventeenth-century literature. One can hardly discover a more widely praised attribute. Baltasar Gracián says, "a discreet silence is the sanctuary of wisdom."[9] Keeping secret a father's murder or a wife's dishonor can be seen easily as discreet wisdom. The lesson of a laudable silence stretches back to antiquity, and by the time of the Renaissance mystic or esoteric silence was displaced by homelier expressions, as in Richard Taverner's version of Erasmus:

> *Stultus stultà loquitur.* A Foole speaketh foolyshe thynges and so our Englyshe proverbe sayeth: a foles bolt is soone shotte, where as the wyseman speaketh seldom and wittily.[10]

Shakespeare shows us Hamlet swearing to secrecy everyone who has seen his father's ghost in an elaborate ritual oath taking, as the characters swear repeatedly upon the cross that is the hilt of Hamlet's sword (in 1.5). *El médico de su honra*'s Don Gutierre becomes obsessive about silence and secrecy, desiring even to keep the insult he must avenge from becoming public knowledge, while planning to take his revenge in a secret and silent manner:

> Y así os receta y ordena
> el médico de su honra
> primeramente la dieta
> del silencio, que es guardar
> la boca.
> [2.656–60]

> Thus the physician of his own honor
> prescribes and orders a diet of silence,
> that is to guard the mouth [keep it closed].

His preoccupation with keeping secret his prescribed vengeance becomes clearer in his act-ending lines:

> Pues médico me llamo de mi honra,
> yo cubriré con tierra mi deshonra.
> [2.1031–32]

> Then physician I call myself of my own honor,
> I shall cover my dishonor with the earth.

He will repeat the metaphor in the next act (3.898–99) in describing his forthcoming vengeance on Mencía, his wife: the earth will keep his secret.

The short step—from attempting to keep the crime hidden while suffering the obligation to avenge it to dissimulating while waiting for the time to act—is taken as both heroes declare the necessity of adopting excessively prudential behavior. Hamlet pretends to be mad, while Don Gutierre stoops to spying on his own wife. Hamlet's decision to accept the ghost's "commandment" (1.5.102) is followed immediately by more than the oath of secrecy (1.5.149). He continues:

> Here, as before, never, so help you mercy,
> How strange or odd soe'er I bear myself—
> As I perchance hereafter shall think meet
> To put an antic disposition on—
> That you, at such times seeing me, never shall,
> . . . . . . . . . . . . . . . .
>                                                    note
> That you know aught of me this not to do,
> So grace and mercy at your most need help you.[11]
> [1.5.177–81, 186–88]

The "antic disposition" is clearly Hamlet's move to accomplish at least two things: find an outlet by which to vent his mounting frustration, and seek a means to fool Claudius into accepting him as harmless. He succeeds in the first endeavor but fails in the second. And, while his pretended madness may seem extreme, moral compendia of the time teem with advice to behave craftily. To cite only a few examples, Erasmus, who can hardly be considered an extreme or radical thinker, proposes:

> *Cretiza cum Cretensi.* Practyse craft wyth the craftie. Of the vanitie and dissimulation of the Cretians thapostle Paule also speketh. This proverbe byddeth us otherwise to dissemble wyth dissemblers, namely where Singlnes woe take no place. The english proverbe sayth: He had nede to have a longe spone that shuld eate with the devyl, meanynge, that he which must have to do with craftye persones ought hymselfe to know crafte.[12]

This kind of deceit, for that is surely what it is, we find countenanced ubiquitously, and not always under the umbrella of "reason of state." Machiavelli invented nothing new. With such advice spread throughout contemporary Christian literature, both Catholic and Protestant, the argument became fundamentally important to the hero caught up in an honor or revenge tragedy. In fact, it proved to be the basic appeal for rationalizing action that would otherwise be understood as unethical. The English

Puritan, William Perkins, writes that scripture provides ample evidence of "that which we commonly [after Machiavelli] call Policie."[13] While he cites Joshua, Rahab, and St. Paul, Diego Saavedra Fajardo, a widely read Spanish compiler of Emblems, cites David and even Christ, "The Master of Truth," to the point of justifying "Dissimulation and cunning . . . not with a design to cheat, but to secure ones self, and prevent being cheated, and for there lawful ends."[14] Finally, and perhaps most succinctly, the Jesuit critic and moralist Baltasar Gracián concludes, "Candor flourished in the Golden Age; in this Iron Age cunning is supreme."[15]

Hamlet's prudent behavior extends to observing Claudius during the play-within-the-play. During this performance the strain and tension build up in the hero, his excitement reaching a high pitch in a scene-ending soliloquy:

> 'Tis now the very witching time of night,
> When churchyards yawn and hell itself breathes out
> Contagion to this world. Now could I drink hot blood,
> And do such bitter business as the day
> Would quake to look on.
> [3.2.379–83]

He closes, promising to heed the ghost's admonition not to harm his mother. He has now gained knowledge enough to confirm the villain's guilt. If his initial problems had to do with keeping his father's murder secret, and his next was how to confirm the guilt of the accused murderer, his next dilemma to solve will be how and when to act.

Prudent, calculating wisdom has satisfied the rational, intellectual side of himself that needed proof. The following scene, when he retreats from killing Claudius at prayer, fearing that his uncle's soul will go to heaven, does not so much test his resolve, but reveals instead the profound feeling seething below that rational, conscious level of prudent activity that both contains and masks his unconscious rage. But the same quality of mind that produced the craftiness to survive also invents otherwise unethical strategies, such as the lying and spying that the social code has come to accept as permissible when open, above-board behavior would not only be unproductive but downright life-threatening.

Hamlet swears his friends to secrecy and asserts his own "antic disposition." Whereas his behavior changes radically, appearing to his on-stage audience to be quite mad (see 2.2), Don Gutierre preserves the grave demeanor of a sober aristocrat. His dissimulation appears especially bizarre in comparison to Hamlet's, perhaps because Don Gutierre sees no opportunity for displaying any antic behavior. He decides to spy upon his wife. In act 2, he enters his own garden not directly through the gate but as if vaulting a low wall *(como saltando unas tapias)*. "In the mute silence of the night . . . in secret I have returned to my house." (En el mudo silencio / de la noche . . . de secreto he venido / hasta mi casa, 2.845, 49–50). He awakens his sleeping wife, allowing her to think that he is Prince Enrique. She warns him to be careful of her husband, who is about to return. Nearly beside himself with rage, and barely able to contain himself, he exits and reenters immediately. Pretending to have just arrived, he shouts a greeting to his wife, this time as her husband.

*Don Gut.* ¡Bella Mencía!

Beautiful Mencía!

*Doña Men.* ¡Oh mi esposo, mi bien y gloria mía!
*(Ap.)* ¡Qué fingidos extremos!
Mas, alma y corazón, disimulemos.

[2.967–70]

Oh my husband, my good and
glorious husband.
*(Aside)* What extreme pretense!
But heart and soul,
we must dissimulate.

He will dissimulate even further. Next he consults the king, explaining that he suspects the Infante, the king's brother, of attempting to seduce his wife. He feigns belief in her honesty, stressing that he has only suspicions. (Ironically he is right, but by this time he is so worked up that he cannot recognize the aptness of his own words; mistrust is as far advanced as it is in *Othello,* although Don Gutierre, like Leontes in *The Winter's Tale,* is his own Iago.) The king, cooperating with the intrigue, allows Don Gutierre to witness the testing of the Infante. Thus from behind a screen[16] Don Gutierre hears what he takes to be an admission of adultery with Mencía. His next move—and his last—will be the cunning and terrible vengeance against his wife.

Events continue to play fortuitously (apparently) into Hamlet's hands. First the players' arrival provided him with the opportunity for gaining proof of Claudius's guilt. Next, plans to send him to England have sped Hamlet out of Denmark after he murders Polonius. Later, we learn how he has been able to save his own life, when he tells Horatio of dispatching Claudius's agents, Rosencrantz and Guildenstern. Cunning has saved Hamlet's life. He relates how he searched the cabin of his companions and discovered Claudius's commission, which would have had him killed. He substituted his own message to countermand his uncle's and resealed the packet.

Following the secrecy and dissimulating, the next step for the revenge and honor hero is to wait for the propitious moment to strike. When that occasion finally arrives, the hero makes the most of his opportunity. Dramaturgically, this occasion might be said to be that point which marks the end of the *epitasis* and the beginning of the *catastrophe*. The action initiated at this proper time will result in the brutal, bloody and tragic spectacle that marks *Hamlet* and *El médico de su honra*.

Like admonitions for a sagacious silence, commonplaces regarding "occasion" are endlessly reiterated. Erasmus, as usual, expresses the paramount importance of the concept in homely, but incisive, language:

> *Nosce tempus.* Knowe Tyme. Opportunitie is of such force that of honest it maketh unhonest, of dammage, avauntage, of pleasure grevaunce, of a good turne a shrewed turne, and contraryewyse of unhonest honest, of avauntage dammage, and brefly to conclude it cleane chaungeth the nature of thynges. This opportunitie or occasion (for so also ye maye call it) in aventurynge and finishynge a busynes: Doubtles beareth the chief stroke, so that not withoute good skyll the paynymes of olde tyme counted it a divine thynge.[17]

In another place Erasmus points out that "you will find very few who follow this proverb *(festina lente)* and rightly combine promptness at the opportune moment with cautious deliberation." Yet he advises one "to hasten, but in such a way that you do not anticipate the appointed time."[18] For Hamlet and Don Gutierre, the ability to recognize occasion is imperative.

Appropriately enough, Gracián uses the topic of occasion to include the previous *topoi* examined above:

> To know how to yield to the times is to surpass them: the man who gets his own way never loses his reputation; when you lack power, use cunning; [get on] somehow or other, either by the highway of merit or the byway of artifice. Craft has achieved more than power and the wise have overcome the brave more often than the brave the wise.[19]

In the same manner, Saavedra Fajardo explicity links together delay, prudence, and occasion in a manner curiously relevant to Don Gutierre especially:

When Time favours, it is assisted by delay . . . nothing is more apposite to prudence, than haste and Passion. Impetuousness ever miscarries, and Examination and Attention are confounded by it . . . Nevertheless, Delay must not be to great, as to let slip the Opportunity of Execution.[20]

Late in act 2, Don Gutierre, trying to suppress his rage at his wife as she speaks to him thinking that he is Prince Enrique, encapsulates neatly the *topoi* of the plot, at the same time revealing the lengths to which the honor hero is prepared to go:

> [*Ap.*] ¿Habrá en el mundo quien paciencia tenga?
> Sí, si prudente alcanza
> oportuna ocasión a su venganza.
> [2.938–40]

> [*Aside*] Is there in the world anyone who
> could hear this and contain himself
> in patience? Yes, there is one such—
> if cautiously he measures the
> occasion for sudden vengeance.

In the next act, he begs for that occasion to reveal itself:

> ¿Para cuándo, para cuándo
> esos azules viriles
> guardan un rayo? No es tiempo
> de que sus puntas se vibren,
> preciando de tan piadosos?
> [3.273–77]

> For when, for when, do you postpone
> your lighting, You powerful azure
> Heavens? Is it not time You shot
> your bolts of lightning, being famous
> for pity, as you are?

By the end of the play, instead of a thunderbolt a cruel quiet deed will dispatch Doña Mencía, preserving the honor of her husband.

Hamlet recognizes occasion, seeing in it also the hand of Providence. While recounting his discovery of Claudius's commission and how he rewrote it, then resealed the packet, Horatio asks, "How was this sealed?" Hamlet responds, "Why, even in that was heaven ordinant. / I had my father's signet in my purse, / Which was the model of the Danish seal" (5.2.47–50). This off-stage action, while obviously crucial to the plot, also signals an important reversal in Hamlet's character. Seizing the occasion, he becomes an active agent for the first time since the frustrating interview with his mother when he mistakenly killed Polonious.

He has the advantage of his adversary. Now the time is his. Confidence replaces suspicions and distrust; Hamlet eagerly accepts the forthcoming duel that the cautious Horatio counsels him to avoid.

Both *Hamlet* and *El médico de su honra* end in bloody carnage. To conclude an after-banquet duel, Shakespeare strews four bodies before us, while Calderón stages impressively a muted spectacle: Doña Mencía's corpse upon her blood-soaked bed. But the most significant difference between these two endings lies in the fact that Hamlet has perished in his duty-fulfilling role as the revenger of his father's murder and restorer of his family honor, whereas Don Gutierre survives, ready to remarry after completing his role as the physician of his own honor.

The two catastrophes promote some feelings of sorrow. In *El médico de su honra*, Don Gutierre suggests that the death of his wife has generated some pity: "But why should I now presume to reduce to words such a pitiful misfortune?" (¿Pero para qué presumo / reducir hoy a palabras / tan lastimosas desdichas?, 3.812–14). And in *Hamlet* we hear Horatio ask Fortinbras, "What is it you would see? / If ought of woe or wonder, cease your search" (5.2.367–68). Yet more importantly, even in their differences, both endings stress the identical dramaturgical effect of wonder (or *admiratio*), probably the most sought after audience emotion by late sixteenth- and seventeenth-century dramatists.[21] The barbaric justice of such violence may not have been applauded wholeheartedly by Shakespeare's or Calderón's spectators, but on-stage interpretation is unambiguous in underscoring the significance of these final moments. Horatio will clarify the circumstances leading to the catastrophe. He will explain publicly to Fortinbras and the others what has happened:

> Give order that these bodies
> High on a stage be placed to the view,
> And let me speak to the yet unknowing world
> How these things came about. So shall you hear
> Of carnal, bloody, and unnatural acts,
> Of accidental judgments, casual slaughters,
> Of deaths put on by cunning and forc'd cause,
> And, in the upshot, purposes mistook
> Fall'n on th' inventors' heads.
>
> [5.2.382–90]

This telling is necessary on at least two grounds; we recall that Hamlet has kept his friend from suicide in order to "Report me and my cause aright / To the unsatisfied" (5.2.344–45). Hamlet needs to have his name cleared of any guilt for having poisoned Claudius. He also wants it known that he has thereby avenged his father's murder. In addition, Horatio wants the story told soon, "lest more mischance / On plots and errors happen" (5.2.399–400). Shakespeare's finale may indeed generate questions. Was Hamlet's mission worth the kingdom of Denmark (now part of Norway, ruled by Fortinbras), the deaths of Polonius, Laertes, and Ophelia, the off-stage executions of Rosencrantz and Guildenstern, and his mother's demise in addition to his own? Has corruption been so thorough that Denmark deserved this kind of near-apocalyptic destruction, providentially ordained by an angry God?

In Spain, however, the catastrophe is private, the tragedy personal. Don Gutierre is the focus. In perhaps the most notorious example of bloodletting in the name of honor, Don Gutierre has hired Ludovico, a barber-surgeon. He blindfolds the surgeon, introduces him to his patient, directs him to bleed her, then orders him to say nothing about this to anyone. Ludovico relates the story of his ministrations to an unknown woman. Presently the king understands that it is Don Gutierre who has engineered the death of his own wife. His reaction is interesting:

> [*Ap.*] Gutierre sin duda es
> el cruel que anoche hizo
> una acción tan inclemente.
> No sé qué hacer. Cuerdamente
> sus agravios satisfizo.
>
> [3.741–45]

> [*Aside*] Undoubtedly Gutierre is the cruel man
> who brought about the unmerciful act
> last night. I do not know what to
> do. He satisfied his insult so cautiously.

After Doña Mencía's lifeless body is revealed, the king notes:

> ¡Notable suceso! [*Ap.* Aquí
> la prudencia es de importancia.
> Mucho en reportarme haré.
> Tomo notable venganza.)
> Cubrid ese horror que asombra,
> ese prodigio que espanta,
> espectáculo que admira,
> símbolo de la desgracia.
>
> [3.824-31]

> What a notable matter! (*Aside*. Here
> prudence is of great importance I
> must restrain my feelings. He took
> a notable vegeance.) Cover this
> horror that astonishes, this prodigy
> that frightens, [this] spectacle that
> awes, [this] symbol of misfortune.

The king thus praises the execution, reenforcing the vital tenet of the honor code that Don Gutierre himself had used to rationalize a course of action that must seem insane. Now the king's own prudence must mark his behavior.

Doña Leonor has by this time appeared conveniently. Earlier, the king had promised to restore her honor, since she had been jilted by Don Gutierre before his unfortunate marriage to his late wife. The finale becomes chilling. Against the backdrop of one wife, now dead, Don Gutierre is given another. He has acted successfully as the physician of his own honor, washing away dishonor's stain with Doña Mencía's innocent blood. Simultaneously and unwittingly he prepares himself for another cure: the restoration of Doña's Leonor's honor through another marriage. The king himself now seizes the occasion to bring about a kind of dramaturgical closure by fulfilling his promise to Doña Leonor. He puts her in the hands of Don Gutierre, who pledges grimly not to forget that he is the physician of his own honor. She accepts him under his conditions. The king commands Don Gutierre, "Give that hand to Leonor, for I know that your excellence deserves her" (Dádsela, pues, a Leonor; / que yo sé que su alabanza / la merece, 3.892–93). She accepts, inviting him to cure her own honor when it needs it. To end the play and complete the action, Don Gutierre, a surprised and reluctant bridegroom, offers his right hand to her, wrapping things up with the usual phrase aimed at the audience. Ironies, of course, abound in the final tableau as the plot lines converge almost too neatly. Audiences are right to sense deep irony by Calderón, but this irony is only part of the powerful impact created by the drama.

Don Gutierre's means of solving his dilemma certainly astonishes, as the king says, but considerable uneasiness accompanies the audience's amazement. A perturbation *(turbación)* of the spirit, *Siglo de Oro* critics call it,[22] and the sources of that discomfort should be explored. Whereas Hamlet's tragic death symbolizes synechdochically the end of Denmark, Don Gutierre's survival and remarriage contrasts metonymically, suggesting not conclusion but continuation. In the popular theater, Calderón has been able to recreate a communal experience felt privately by members of his audience.

Don Gutierre simultaneously represents and embodies the haunting honor code, whose unrelenting laws threaten seventeenth-century Spaniards. Safely distanced aesthetically upon a stage, conveniently estranged in time, Don Gutierre follows perfectly the honor code's stipulations that by themselves in other contexts make considerable good sense. However, when they crystalize as procedures followed to ensure the male ego's defense of its reputation at all costs, otherwise reasonable virtues are suddenly made ironic. Calderón demonstrates that the secrecy, suffering, and dissimulation followed deliberately by the hero while waiting for the opportunity to bring about a culminating bloodletting make up more than the casual ingredients of a plot designed to compound suspense and supply sensational theatrics. Besides functioning as apparent adventitious, formulaic story elements, more fundamentally they constitute aspects of a deep psychic reality, fusing together facets of plot and character that focus an audience's attention on profoundly felt ambivalent responses to certain basic ego needs. Culturally and socially, these needs relate to maintaining one's honor.

Within the commercially successful, aesthetically complex, governmentally censored activity of late Renaissance popular theater, Calderón and Shakespeare pack into their dramatic fables profound human responses to an issue that strikes their audiences deeply. In *Hamlet* and *El médico de su honra* the subjects of revenge and honor are first exposed then anatomized in order for their audiences to see their own values initially reflected and finally interpreted. Tragic implications are usually hidden by the aphoristic dialogue spoken in soliloquy by the heroes. Their destructive (if not mad) behavior is rationalized by the *topoi* that advise keeping a discreet silence, acting craftily, and knowing the time.

The mixture of awe and uneasiness found at the end of *El médico de su honra,* the questions we are led to ask about the cost to Hamlet of his successful revenge, point to the irony central to these tragedies. While Hamlet and Don Gutierre maintain their masculine egos through heroic effort, their achievements fail to bring them ultimate success. In the desperate striving to maintain its dignity, indeed its mastery, the male ego in these tragedies subverts itself. Calderón and Shakespeare are using certain dominant social and cultural codes analogously. They neither approve nor condemn popular belief in these codes; instead they put the codes to the test in the popular drama, showing the effect that the codes have on action and character. They, like all great writers, leave it to their audience to determine whatever significance there may be in all of this.

## Notes

1. Quotes from *Hamlet* are from the Arden edition, ed. Harold Jenkins (London: Methuen, 1982).

2. Quotes from the text are from *El médico de su honra,* ed. Angel Valbuena Briones, Clásicos castellanos (Madrid: Espasa-Calpe, 1956). Translations are based on *The Surgeon of His Honour,* trans. Roy Campbell (Madison: University of Wisconsin Press, 1960), but I have tried to make them more literal.

3. See the appendix to John Loftis, *Renaissance Drama in England and Spain: Topical Allusion and History Plays* (Princeton: Princeton University Press, 1987).

4. Walter Cohen, *Drama of a Nation: Public Theater in Renaissance England and Spain* (Ithaca: Cornell University Press, 1985), p. 9.

5. Northrop Frye, *Anatomy of Criticism: Four Essays* (Princeton: Princeton University Press, 1957), p. 171.

6. Georges Duby, *The Knight, The Lady, and The Priest: The Making of Modern Marriage in Medieval France* (New York: Pantheon, 1983), p. 38.

7. A good overview of recent tendencies in scholarship concerning Honor in Spain at this time can be found in Melveena McKendrick, "Honour/Vengeance in the Spanish *Comedia:* A Case of Mimetic Transference," *Modern Language Review* 79 (1984): 313–35.

8. Other discussions of these *topoi* are found in Bruce Golden, "Calderón's Tragedies of Honor: *Topos*, Emblem, and Action in the Popular Theater of the *Siglo de Oro*," *Renaissance Drama*, N.S. 3 (1971): 239–62 and "The Authority of Honor in Lope's *El castigo sin venganza*," in *Shakespeare and Dramatic Tradition: Essays in Honor of S. F. Johnson*, ed. W. R. Elton and William B. Long, forthcoming from the University of Delaware Press.

9. Baltasar Gracián, *The Oracle: A Manual of the Art of Discretion (Oraculo manual y arte de prudencia),* trans. L. B. Walton (New York: Dutton, 1962) pp. 50–51.

10. *Proverbs or Adagies gathered out of the Chiliades of Erasmus,* by R. Taverner (London, 1539), Sig. iii$^r$.

11. I have followed Kittredge in keeping line 187 from the Second Quarto.

12. *Proverbs or Adagies gathered out of the Chiliades of Erasmus, by Richard Taverner, with new additions as well of Latyn proverbs as of English* (London, 1545), Sig. lx$^{r-v}$.

13. William Perkins, *The Whole Treatise of the Case of Conscience, Works*, vol. 2 (London, 1631), p. 116.

14. Diego Saavedra Fajardo, *Idea de un príncipe político cristiano* (Madrid, 1640); quoted from the English version by Sir John Astry, *The Royal Politician* (London, 1700) pp. 306–7.

15. Gracián, *The Oracle,* pp. 216–17.

16. In his palace, the Escorial, Philip II had a secret room constructed from which he could observe palace inhabitants through a grating. This grave and prudent king might be a good touchstone for *Siglo de Oro* audiences. See Garrett Mattingly, *The Armada* (Boston: Houghton & Mifflin, 1959), p. 73. The frequency of the topic in the manuals, and its application by sympathetic protagonists, vitiates criticism by Fredson Bowers (in *Elizabethan Revenge Tragedy* [1940; reprint ed., Gloucester, Mass.: Peter Smith, 1959, pp. 80ff.] who asserts "the English insistence on straightforward action"), Alfred Harbage, "Intrigue in Elizabethan Tragedy," *Essays on Shakespeare and Elizabethan Drama* (Columbia: University of Missouri Press, 1962, pp. 27–44), and Ruth Nevo, who claims, mistakenly, I would say,

"Prudence, however, is generally recognized by Elizabethans as a Machiavellian vice" in "All-in-All Sufficiency in *Othello*," *Shakespeare Studies* 6 (1972): 221, n. 7.

17. Erasmus-Taverner, 1545, Sig. xxiv$^v$–xxv$^r$.

18. Margaret Mann Phillips, *The "Adages" of Erasmus* (Cambridge: Cambridge University Press, 1964), p. 174.

19. Gracián, *The Oracle*, pp. 216–17.

20. Saavedra Fajardo, *The Royal Politician*, p. 442.

21. *Admiratio* has been discussed widely, but a good place to begin is still J. V. Cunningham, *Woe or Wonder: The Emotional Effect of Shakespearean Tragedy* (1951); reprinted in *Tradition and Poetic Structure* (Denver, Colo.: Swallow, 1960).

22. *Turbación* has also been taken into account by critics and scholars; see, e.g., E. C. Riley, "The Dramatic Theories of Don Jusepe Antonio Gonzalez de Salas," *Hispanic Review* 19 (1951): 183–203.

# Elemental Ambiguity in *El hijo del sol, Faetón* and *The Tempest*

Denise M. DiPuccio
*University of Tennessee*

ANY number of conventional approaches could provide the framework for a comparative analysis of Calderón's *El hijo del sol, Faetón* (1661) and Shakespeare's *The Tempest* (1611). A character study reveals similarities in the protagonists' efforts to claim their rightful titles. Prospero, usurped Duke of Milan, wants to retrieve his domain; Phaethon, son of Apollo, longs for recognition as a demi-god. A thematic comparison leads to more abstract generalizations about individuals' struggles for control and to what end they use that power. An even broader thematic comparison taps the allegorical potential of the plays. Seen in this light, the works make comparable statements on nature, cycles, births, and deaths. One could also focus on Calderón's and Shakespeare's style and language. Both plays, written late in the playwrights' careers, reflect marked stylistic differences from earlier plays. A more technical analysis could examine the elaborate stage settings of these plays. As representative courtly drama of Golden Age Spain and Elizabethan/Jacobean England, both pieces incorporate advanced staging techniques. Each of these points of departure, although valid, is peripheral to a more basic parallel. The most intriguing comparative point hinges on the strange things that occur in the plays and the characters' inability to decipher their meaning.

These astonishing events are more than flights of fancy that invite the audience to escape from a dreary reality and that allow Shakespeare and Calderón to strut undeniable intellectual and artistic talent. Both playwrights structure their plots around religious and philosophical beliefs that prove man's continued attempts to explain the enigmatic facets of the world. The very title of Calderón's drama promises to stage an amazing event derived from classical mythology. The source of strangeness in *The Tempest* is a bit more obscure for a contemporary audience. Nevertheless, as Karol Berger explains, the Renaissance attitude toward spiritual magic was comparable to the twentieth-century attitude toward psychoanalysis.[1] Robert West further notes that "Ariel and his elves and Prospero's magic were literally intended."[2] Both classical mythology and magic were the subject of numerous Renaissance and Neoplatonic treatises. Scholars and theologians reworked these concepts along lines compatible with Christian doctrine.[3] By adding a didactic touch to the classical tales and by distinguishing white from black magic, scholars could justifiably incorporate these otherwise heretical ideas into their own dogmas. The fact that Calderón and Shakespeare deal with extratextual credos broadens the implications of the plays. The audience can easily dismiss pure fantasy as irrelevant to reality. Nevertheless, a play that deals with the structured beliefs of a people encourages even the most skeptical viewer to deliberate the implications of the strange events of the plays.

The characters and the spectator confront enigmatic situations that play havoc with their perceptions of reality. Each of these mysteries, caused by the Olympians' supernatural powers or Prospero's awesome magic, challenges the characters to explain the unexplainable. The characters frequently mention the four elements in their descriptions of puzzling events. The need to determine the role played by fire, air, earth, and water in their lives prevails in the characters' dialogues. Furthermore, the stage settings visually stress the omnipresent elements.

A brief overview on the conceptualization of the elements introduces some of the sources from which these seventeenth-century playwrights drew their material. Although Calderón and Shakespeare had the background, ability, and opportunity to study philosophical literature dealing with the four elements, neither one had to do so. They incorporated into their works widespread interpretations of what began with the ancients' account of creation. Ovid explains that a supreme being ordered the world:

> So things evolved, and out of blind confusion
> Found each its place, bound in eternal order.
> The force of fire, that weightless element,
> Leaped up and claimed the highest place in heaven;
> Below it, air; and under them the earth
> Sank with its grosser portions; and the water,
> Lowest of all, held up, held in, the land.
> [*Metamorphoses* 1.25–31]

Ovid summarizes two principles that figure in classical, medieval, and Renaissance perceptions of the elements in the cosmos: order and hierarchy. Subsequent philosophers refine and elaborate on these points. But, as Jack Sage points out, the Neoplatonists did not alter these basics: "The four elements exist in a state of harmony. Should they not, world harmony would be destroyed. The elements form, therefore, the basis of world harmony."[4] Christian philosophers scrutinized more thoroughly the question of whether or not man controls the elements. E. M. Wilson explains the paradoxical relationship between man and the world: "After Man's creation they [the elements] are his servants, but after the Fall he is delivered to them for imprisonment. In a sense they are still his servants, but they are also his gaolers."[5]

To control the elements is the goal of the protagonists of *El hijo del sol, Faetón* and *The Tempest*. Both characters eventually command even the highest element of fire. Phaethon guides the sun; Prospero ignites lightning. Their privileged status ends when the two protagonists forfeit control. In a jealous rage Phaethon unintentionally steers his chariot off course; Prospero, in resolute calm, decides to drown his book of magic. In each instance, water, the basest element, destroys the devices with which the characters manipulated their environments: the chariot and the book.

Both plays stress the physical, intellectual, and, most importantly, linguistic change that transform mortals into supermen. Calderón and Shakespeare establish language as the key to understanding and controlling the world. The characters with the most advanced verbal skills govern the elements and cause events that confound everyone else. Those with inferior linguistic resources try to familiarize the strangeness by defining it in terms they know. These aspects of the plays reflect what Gayle Greene defines as "the early Renaissance ideal of language as expression of the rational and civilized, with creative power analogous to that of the Word."[6] Apparently, the more articulate one becomes, the more privy (s)he is to the secrets of the universe.

Nevertheless, linguistic competence becomes a liability when it amplifies, and therefore complicates, the possible definitions of reality. The playwrights give equal attention to the characters' failures to grasp cosmic harmony through language. All of the characters rely on language that confuses, hides, and shades meaning. Two factors inhibit effective communciation and interpretation: the complexity of what they see or hear and the inadequacy of signs to communicate that event. These qualities underscore the difference between an event and the characters' attempts to interpret its meaning.[7] Hence, they grossly misinterpret and then exchange their misinterpretations.

Two conflictive arguments, then, undermine each other

throughout the plays: language leads to cosmic awareness; the arbitrary and deficient nature of language precludes that outcome. This tension simultaneously draws the characters nearer to and further from the order of the universe. Equivocal communication also destabilizes cosmic harmony itself. The elements fall prey to vague language because their own visual and verbal signs delude meaning. Natural disasters, when one element pits itself against another, obviously signify confusion. Yet, nature in its calmest repose belies inherent contentions. The elements reflect and are reflected by harmony as well as discord. Furthermore, no linguistic key deciphers the heavily encoded elements. As a result, the elusive strangeness defers, until some future time, the forfeiture of its complexity.[8] The supposed harmony that the characters want to understand remains a potential, steeped, for the moment, in linguistic ambiguity.

The action of *El hijo del sol, Faetón* traces a shepherd's discovery that he is Apollo's son, his desire to prove that noble parentage to skeptical peers, and his attempts to win the sun god's recognition. The protagonist journeys to the heavens, where, in a moment of Olympian sovereignty, he guides the sun across the sky. Nevertheless, Phaethon loses control of his chariot and steers it too close to earth. Realizing the potential danger, Phaethon drives the fiery vehicle into the river Eridanus, thereby destroying himself and the fire. As the protagonist rises through the elements, he suffers a series of linguistic metamorphoses that complement his physical location in the cosmos and his heightened intellectual capacities. The loftier the element he inhabits, the more resources Phaethon taps to communicate. When he reaches the sun, he also reaches his linguistic peak. This culmination, however, is temporary and the protagonist loses whatever cosmic awareness he gains en route to the heavens.

Even before Phaethon deals specifically with the more complex higher elements, he battles with prosaic, but confusing, earthly and marine events. In fact, the secondary characters envelop Phaethon in an atmosphere where communicative breakdown is the norm. A blatant example of the characters' equivocal use of language and misinterpretation of events occurs near the beginning of the play. King Admeto tried and failed to capture and slay a wild animal that stalks the forest and harrasses Sicily's inhabitants. When Silvia, a peasant girl, attempts to narrate Admeto's adventure, the jester, Batillo, constantly interrupts her. Although this event is of minor importance to the plot, it introduces the linguistic problems developed in the play and suggests that an apparently simple mundane occurrence befuddles the characters as much as any celestial phenomenon:

>Sil. ... Admeto, rey de Tesalia ...
>Bat. ... Tesalia Admeto de rey ...
>Sil. ... de su valor persuadido ...
>Bat. ... se valor suadido per ...
>
>. . . . . . . .
>
>Sil. ... fue al amancecer a caza.
>Bat. ... fue a caza al amanecer.
>
>. . . . . . . .
>
>Sil. ... en la red cayó la fiera.
>Bat. ... cayó en la fiera la red.
>Sil. Romperla pudo feroz ...
>Bat. La feroz pudo romper ...
>
>. . . . . . . .
>
>Sil. Y haciendo dos mil estragos ...
>Bat. Tragos mil haciendo y cien ...[9]
>
>Sil. ... Admeto, king of Thessaly ...
>Bat. ... Thessaly Admeto of king ...
>Sil. ... convinced of his valor ...
>Bat. ... ho valor vinced con ...
>
>. . . . . . . .
>
>Sil. ... went at dawn to the hunt.
>Bat. ... went to the hunt at dawn.
>
>. . . . . . . .
>
>Sil. ... the beast fell in the net.
>Bat. ... the net fell on the beast.
>Sil. He managed to break it fiercely ...
>Bat. The fierce beast managed to break ...
>
>. . . . . . . .
>
>Sil. ... and causing two thousand damages ...
>Bat. ... making a thousand drinks and hundred ...

Every other line of this exchange, Silvia's narration, relates a logical sequence of events. King Admeto made a valiant attempt to capture the beast. The savage momentarily fell into a net, broke loose, and once again roams the forest. Batillo's description differs from that of the shepherdess and causes more confusion than clarity of details. His narration leads to a series of apparently trivial questions. What is the king's real name? Tesalia? Admeto? Tesalia Admeto? Did the beast fall into the net or did the net fall on the beast? Was the beast drinking heavily or causing tremendous havoc? The answers to these questions seem annoyingly obvious. Silvia's logical description invalidates Batillo's nonsense. This dialogue, however, disrupts communication. Part of the incoherency stems from an uneducated peasant's inadvertent misuse of language. Besides exposing Batillo's humorous inability to speak and to hear Spanish correctly, these passages reveal underlying ambiguities in language. Acceptable linguistic deviations, such as colloquialisms, flexible syntax, and double meanings, contribute to the impenetrability of Batillo's story. Even knowing the grammatical intricacies does not ensure that two witnesses will interpret the same mundane event in the same way. Language brings communication to a standstill.

Batillo unwittingly, but blatantly, communicates poorly. As the play develops, subtler and more serious incidences reveal the tenuous effectiveness of language. While communication is not paralyzed, it is more complex. For example, Clymene, Phaethon's mother, intentionally misleads with ambiguous language. Clad in animal skins in order to hide her identity, Clymene is the "beast" that escaped from Admeto's net. When Phaethon captures her, Clymene begs for her life while trying to conceal her true identity. This predicament forces Clymene to speak more artfully than the other characters. Because she is guarding a secret but does not want to lie to her son, Clymene concerns herself with the way she speaks as much as with what she says. She implicates more than she states. When she calls Phaethon "all my good and . . . all my misfortune" (todo mi bien y . . . todo mi mal, 1869b), she confuses her son. Clymene's verbal duplicity challenges Phaethon to discover the meaning of her words. He becomes conscious of the fact that manipulative discourse obfuscates more than it clarifies. Furthermore, Clymene forces her son to realize the hidden complexities of an apparently simple rustic life.

The arbitrary nature of language affects not only the characters' fictional dialogues but the spectators' real interaction with the play. This second level of communication widens the breach between events and language. Unlike the characters, who move about in the limited artifice of the stage, the audience has at its disposal extratextual knowledge that makes it possible to interpret events on a level unavailable to the fictional characters. The opening scene of the play, in which everyone awaits the arrival of Thetis, exemplifies these levels of interpretation. This scene also marks the characters' initial attempts to interpret a sign related to an element other than earth. Phaethon describes "that reef, / that is her triumphant carriage" (aquel escollo, / que su triunfal carro es, p. 1863b). The sign "reef" is polysemic. First it functions denotatively and points toward the sea numph's arrival.[10] Phaethon's verbal signs prepare the viewer for the visual spectacle about to appear. This sign also functions connotatively for the characters and the audience. Phaethon symbolically connects the sign "reef" to Thetis' triumphant carriage.[11] Their linkage is arbitrary; a reef and a carriage do not necessarily share similar physical properties that warrant such a comparison.

The shepherd manipulates language in a relatively sophisticated manner to announce Thetis' dramatic entrance. Nevertheless, the audience, taking the symbolism one step further, may link the reef to danger and risk.[12] Therefore, these signs foreshadow the denouement in which water, signified by the Nereid and the river Eridanus, kills the protagonist. The characters' and the public's interpretations of these signs differ. The characters' impressions are not incorrect, but more incomplete. Limited by the context of the play, Phaethon cannot distance himself from his fictional setting to analyze signs in light of prevailing literary codes. Because earth and water comprise part of his familiar surroundings, Phaethon is ironically self-confident that his interpretations of reality are accurate.

When the characters refer to the ethereal elements of air and fire, they lose their ability to speak symbolically and resort to basic communicative processes. Even a sea deity, like Thetis, only acknowledges the sun's function of measuring time: "Let's depart, for the sun is finishing its course" (Vamos, que el sol ya su carrera acaba, p. 1871b). The nymph relies on denotative reasoning to make these statements. She exercises little interpretive ability to talk about the sun.

More acute awareness of the elements of fire and air arises when the protagonist begins to vent his despair over his terrestrial misfortune. Phaethon directs his laments to the higher and incomprehensible element of air and asks, "until when, heavens, / does my life have to be portents? (¿hasta cuándo, cielos, / mi vida ha de ser prodigios?, p. 1876b). The protagonist, however, still makes no explicit connection between air/fire and his good fortune. He addresses the heavens, but does not assume that they will provide a release from misfortune. The protagonist relegates the higher elements to a realm of questions and mysteries. He may address them but he dare not presume to understand them.

Phaethon's heightened desperation in act 2 initiates a change in his communicative endeavors. In a monologue that contrasts another shepherd's recent good fortune with his own adversity, Phaethon reveals a more discriminating perspective of the loftier elements. While the protagonist defines his own existence as "valley," he describes Epaphus' life as "sun." Now a crowned prince, betrothed to Thetis, Epaphus enjoys prestige inaccessible to Phaethon. The protagonist longs to share in some of this good fortune; he wants a part of the sun. When Phaethon begins to equate blessing with fire, his language becomes self-referential. He is conscious of the power of words and describes "the metaphor of the sun" (la metáfora del sol, p. 1880b). Phaethon is now aware of the fact that he uses the sign of fire symbolically; he links fire with luck and hopes that the sun will shed some providential rays on him. Because he still has no idea that he is Apollo's son, Phaethon does not detect the inherent irony of his hopes. He does, however, learn about cryptic words that play an important role in the definition of his complex reality. Before acquiring this awareness, he was content to leave the mystery of the heavens untouched. Equipped with his new linguistic acuteness, Phaethon sets out to decipher the engima.

Yet, for all his linguistic development, Phaethon's encounter with Apollo illustrates another failure in communication. This time the rupture occurs because Phaethon does not listen to a straightforward statement. When Phaethon asks for permission to guide his father's chariot, Apollo explains the potential danger:

> Tan precisa es mi carrera
> . . . . . . . .
>
> que desmandada verás
> que más abrasa que luce
>
> [P. 1897a]
>
> my course is so precise
> . . . . . . . .
>
> that if you stray, you will see
> that it burns more than it shines

Apollo wants to warn his son; he does so correctly, if Delphically. But even the sun god apparently has no idea that his words are prophetic as well as cautionary. Phaethon's unmindful interpretation of Apollo's warning produces drastic consequences.

Phaethon's chariot ride coincides with the final stage of his linguistic development. Ethereal elements now constitute part of the protagonist's cognizant reality. From his celestial coach, Phaethon acquires a new perspective which grants him even more linguistic liberties. He combines signs from ethereal and terrestrial elements in order to create symbols. When he describes the "ethereal fields" (etéreos campos) as a "brilliant vessel of gold" (luciente bajel de oro, p. 1900a), he first connects air to earth and then fire to water. These symbols mark the uppermost point in Phaethon's physical and linguistic journey. His enhanced language complements his physical location, the apogee of the heavens. Phaethon's celestial glory abruptly ends when he diverts his attention to earth. He glances down and sees Epaphus seducing Thetis. The protagonist forgets Apollo's warning, misguides the chariot, sets himself and the earth on fire, and falls into the river Eridanus.

Phaethon's destruction is the result of several communicative failures. Partial decodings of his parents' warnings and his inability to interpret the "reef" as a symbol of danger prevent the protagonist from successfully reigning over the elements. Furthermore, cosmic harmony becomes a suspect theory when the elements, or one of their representatives, cannot impose order and signify discord as often as harmony.

Visual markers on stage complement the protagonist's intellectual and verbal progression through the cosmos.[13] The predominant sign of the first two acts is "forest." The simple stage direction, "the theater will be a forest" (el teatro será de bosque, p. 1863a), establishes not only the terrestrial setting of the act, but the protagonist's verbal and conceptual abilities. The forest limits Phaethon's language and comprehension. While Phaethon changes, so do the sign systems on stage. Visual signs represent the forces that encourage Phaethon to rise. The goddess of the rainbow acts as mediator. Iris expedites Phaethon's journey by placing him on a pyramid so that he is nearer to the sun. The pyramid, which physically elevates Phaethon, signifies the early stages of his linguistic and intellectual ascent. When the audience next sees the hero, he moves about the palace of the sun and stands before Apollo's throne.

Journeys though the elements are as prevalent in *The Tempest* as they are in *El hijo del sol, Faetón*. The characters, however, do not pass vertically from the basest element of water to the highest of fire. When the King of Naples and his entourage drag themselves to the shores of the island, they enter a realm in which the hierarchical structure of the elements has been abolished by Prospero's magic. Fire succumbs to the magician's power as readily as water. And Prospero uses all four elements to stage unnatural spectacles that mesmerize his viewers and challenge them to try to explain just what is going on. Shakespeare, then, focuses on the same issues presented by Calderón: elemental strangeness and finding the words to describe it.

The first scene immediately draws attention to these ideas. The characters battle against the raging sea that eventually shipwrecks them. Greene discusses the characters' attempts to tame the storm through several types of verbal media: "rational discourse, imprecation, injunction, invocation of the king's name, a plea for silence, and, finally, for prayer." The emphasis on words and speech evidences the characters' attempts to control something strange with linguistic patterns that are familiar to them. Their linguistic abilities, however, are no match for the tempest. Greene argues that this scene, and the entire play, exposes "the limits of language before wonder and grace."[14]

Nevertheless, "wonder and grace" are not the only factors that limit language. Familiarity and ease also lock the characters into communicative checkmate. Like the characters of *El hijo del sol, Faetón*, the nobles and the sailors of *The Tempest* feel most comfortable on land, the element with which they are most familiar. Hence, Gonzalo's remark, "I would fain die a dry death,"[15] indicates that he would rather confront unknown death on his own territory. Subsequent conversations and events, however, prove that the ordinary can become unsettlingly foreign.

The following example of strange familiarity occurs during a respite from Prospero's magical distortion of reality, thereby suggesting that mundane elements befuddle the characters as much as ethereal ones. In act 2, the nobles, in an effort to cheer up the king, chat about the island. A conversation on the physical properties of the island elicits some differences of opinion. Gonzalo and Adrian describe it as "lush . . . lusty . . . [and] . . . green" (2.1.55–56); Sebastian and Antonio insist that it is "tawny" (2.1.56). Furthermore, Gonzalo chatters about his garments, which, in spite of the storm, seem fresh and clean. The others respond with sarcastic insults and clever puns. This scene has the same comic tone and apparent triviality of the scene in which Batillo and Silvia recount Admeto's adventure with the beast. Once again, due to the silliness of the conversation, the spectator may not feel compelled to decide what is the exact condition of the character's clothes or how many shrubs grow on the island. Nevertheless, the nobles' dialogue serves a dramatic function similar to the peasants' narration in *El hijo del sol, Faetón*. Several people, describing the same set of mundane circumstances, offer conflicting interpretations. The characters, who acknowledge the fascinating allure of Prospero's magic, seem naively unaware that simple events also intrigue them. They are equally ignorant of the potential of language to change perceptions of reality.

The nobles' humorous discussion introduces a primary visual sign system in the play. Garments and how they look on people are the topic of several conversations which suggest that an interpretation of reality depends on the viewer's perspective. After the royal party debates the (un)stained condition of their robes, Antonio, who usurped his brother's dukedom and now wears ducal garb, says to Sebastian, "look how well my garments sit upon me" (2.1.312). Although Antonio assumes that his outfit is tailor-made, Prospero would like to reclaim the ill-fitting garments. Later in the same act, the drunken jester, Trinculo, shelters himself from the rain by hiding under Caliban's gaberdine (2.2.35–42). The tipsy Stephano then defines the amorphous mass as "some monster . . . with four legs" (2.2.67–68). But the most impressive metamorphosis occurs when Prospero puts on his magician's robe. The usurped duke becomes a supernatural force beyond human redress. Antonio's gown makes him a duke; Caliban's cape shapes a two-legged monster into a four-legged one; Prospero's robes transform him into a magician. Clothes not only make the man, they make him what he is not. This emphasis on clothes further develops the idea that familiar objects may cloak or unveil enigmas that rival even the strangest phenomena.

When magic begins to envelop the characters in ambiguity they lose all their linguistic confidence to explain Prospero's apparent manipulation of the elements. The two most detailed examples of Prospero's magic are the banquet and the masque. The magician uses these visual spectacles for two purposes: the banquet leads to the repentance of those who stole his dukedom; the masque blesses the forthcoming marriage of Miranda, his daughter, to Ferdinand, the Prince of Naples. Both rituals reduce the other characters to linguistic simpletons. The King of Naples and his men ask questions when they hear music and see strange shapes bringing in an elaborate feast: "What harmony is this? . . . What were these?" (3.3.25–27). After this initial questioning they define the shapes in recognizable, yet imprecise, terms: "a living drollery . . . people of the island" (3.3.28–39). The characters try to mold the strangeness into something they know. Ferdinand reacts with similar naiveté to the enchanting masque. His ingenuous questions and exclamations, "May I be bold to think these spirits? . . . Let me live here ever!" (4.1.132–36), indicate his awe. Miranda, for whom such wonders have become the norm, reacts with no surprise.

Prospero's magical productions rival the mythological extravaganzas of *El hijo del sol, Faetón*. Nevertheless, unlike Calderón, who reworks a specific Ovidian tale, Shakespeare taps several classical and Renaissance sources for *The Tempest*.[16] Elements of Longus's *Daphne and Chloe,* Ayrer's *Die Schöne Sidea,* the improvisational *scenari* of the commedia dell arte, and Montaigne's concept of the "noble savage" surface in *The Tempest*.[17] Specific mythological figures, however, do have a role in Shakespeare's romance. During the banquet, Ariel becomes a harpy who chastizes Antonio and Alonso for their past deceits. The harpy then makes the feast disappear before ravenous men have a chance to eat. Ariel's role and actions recall Vergil's harpies who scolded Aeneas and his crew for stealing their food.[18] Later, during the masque, spirits, in the forms of mythological goddesses and nymphs, appear on stage. Prospero, seated at the top, presides over a reunion among Juno, Ceres, and Iris. Although *The Tempest* is a romance, its mythological features add another layer of strangeness to the play.[19] From the perspective of the other characters, the magus has at his beck and call the Queen of Olympus, the goddess of plenty, the goddess of the rainbow, as well as assorted oreads and nereids.

It would seem, then, that Shakespeare has taken his protagonist one step further than Calderón. Although Phaethon gradually deepens his understanding of the elements and momentarily controls them, he is killed by the sea. Prospero, on the other hand, masters the elements over an extended period of time. When the play begins, he has already reached the intellectual and linguistic peak toward which Phaethon strives throughout *El hijo del sol, Faetón*. Prospero has learned the magic words which grant him the power to flash lightning, shake the earth, move the air, and rile the sea. Shakespeare honors the secrecy of this linguistic code by not revealing the contents of the magic book. The audience sees Prospero's robe and staff but never hears the words that mobilize the elements. At any rate, Prospero's magic, be it Ficinian, theurgic, pneumatologic, demonic, or white, makes him privy to the secrets of the universe.[20] The mortal has apparently surpassed the power of the semi-god.

Several factors, however, qualify Prospero's supposed omnipotence. The mortals believe that harpies, goddesses, and nymphs obey Prospero's commands. The characters do not know that elves and "demipuppets," under Prospero's direction, adopt the roles of Iris, Ceres, and Juno. It is *as if* the mythological figures graced the island. No one can deny Prospero's magical power to stage amazing spectacles. This magic, however, substitutes the real thing. The artificial quality of Prospero's masque forces us to reconsider other examples of his magic. Does Prospero magically create the illusion of controlling the elements or does he magically control them? Both phenomena have the same effect; they startle everyone else. Yet, the question does undermine Prospero's apparent authority. Furthermore, trying to discover the real domain of Prospero's magic underscores the linguistic problems of the play. It opens the gap between an event and an interpretation of that event.

Yet another factor restricts the magician's power. Prospero develops interdependent relationships with the objects of his control. Ariel, Prospero's spiritual stage manager, makes sure that the others learn their lines, organizes the props, and gives the actors their cues. Ariel is an indispensable slave. Prospero has ultimate control over the spirit, but without Ariel Prospero's elaborate productions would be theatrical failures.

The second relationship involves the protagonist and one of the elements, the sea. At the end of the play, Prospero voluntarily relinquishes his magical powers in order to retrieve his ducal command. In one of his final monologues, Prospero enumerates the wonders he created in the past and plans to destroy his power. In addition to breaking his staff and shedding his robe, Prospero declares, "I'll drown my book" (5.1.64). This statement brings the element of water to full circle in the play. In the opening scene, helpless mariners battled against the tempest; Prospero now willingly puts his magic at the mercy of the sea. Until he completes this process, he masters the element. Prospero will drown, not be drowned. Yet, in the moment that he immerses his book, the divested magician loses sovereignty. The sea will destroy the magical incantations. Prospero, in turn, becomes a potential victim of future tempests. Prospero does not immediately die when he relinquishes his magic. Unlike Phaethon, whose loss of control coincided with his drowning, Prospero has a future; he will return to Milan. Yet, the duke envisions a grim future: "Every third thought shall be my grave" (5.1.365). No language can help either protagonist control the most common and the most enigmatic mystery of all.

In *El hijo del sol, Faetón* and *The Tempest* Calderón and Shakespeare pose similar questions about using language to make sense out of reality. The unresolved tension of both plays centers on whether or not the characters will be able to define strange events that puzzle them. Two dramatic genuises have earned the critical right to ask this question. Long literary careers awakened their sensitivity to the advantages and the drawbacks of linguistic command. Like their protagonists, they mastered language and, as a result, created intrigue. Their creations, like those of their fictional counterparts, challenge the critic to find a key to the mystery. Nevertheless, they steer the critic away from that goal by deliberately exposing the process of creating ambiguity and by explicitly underscoring the enigma of their own texts. This ambiguity is, in part, a product of Baroque orientations. Chronological and artistic classifications, however, limit the timelessness and modernity of classics. Two seventeenth-century artistic works preempt twentieth-century critical trends to dismantle logic in the text. They lay bare examples of the arbitrary nature of language and its effects on comprehension of cosmic harmony. They anachronistically put into practice post-Saussurian and post-structuralist theory. This chronological merging bodes well for the practice and the theory. Not only does it strengthen the bond between art and criticism, it attests to the endurance of both. Canonical literature, like *El hijo del sol, Faetón* and *The Tempest*, becomes strange when twentieth-century criticism defamiliarizes its seventeenth-century content. Revolutionary concepts, like deconstruction, become conventional when three-hundred-year-old texts foreground their differences and deferrals.

## Notes

1. Karol Berger, "Prospero's Art," *Shakespeare Studies*, vol. 3, ed. J. Leeds Barroll (New York: Burt, Franklin, 1977), p. 212.

2. Robert H. West, *Shakespeare & the Outer Mystery* (Lexington: University Press of Kentucky, 1968), p. 81.

3. In Spain, Calderón was probably familiar with the work which best represents this fusion of classical and Christian traditions, Pérez de Moya's *Philosophia secreta* (Madrid, 1585); reprinted in Eduardo Gómez Baquero, ed., *Los clásicos olvidados*, vols. 1 and 2 (Madrid: Nueva Biblioteca de Autores Españoles, 1928). On the other hand, Shakespeare was probably aware of the trend to rework magic along Christian lines. West points out that several Platonists tried to combine the two traditions: "Platonistic writers like Ficino and Cornelius Agrippa strain to find Christian warrant for pagan-ideas, and orthodox Catholic writers often accommodate data that we might suppose essentially alien to their theology." See *Shakespeare & the Outer Mystery*, p. 57.

4. Jack Sage, "The Function of Music in the Theatre of Calderón," in *The Comedias of Calderón*, vol. 19, ed. D. W. Cruickshank and J. E. Varey (London: Gregg, 1973), p. 212.

5. E. M. Wilson, "The Four Elements in the Imagery of Calderón," *Modern Language Review* 31 (1936): 192. Hans Flasche, in his article, "Más detalles sobre el papel de los

cuatro elementos en la obra de Calderón," *Letras de Deusto* 11 (julio-diciembre 1981): 5–14, also discusses several Latin and Greek texts that theorize on elemental order and man's relationship to the elements. Although Flasche focuses primarily on the *autos sacramentales*, some of his observations are applicable to Calderón's secular drama.

6. Gayle Greene, "'Excellent Dumb Discourse': Silence and Grace in Shakespeare's *Tempest*," *Studia Neophilologica* 50 (1978): 197.

7. G. Douglas Atkins summarizes Derrida's idea of difference: "Because the sign, phonic as well as graphic, is a structure of difference, signs being made possible through the differences between sounds, that which is signified by the signifier is never present in and of itself. As a result, word and thing, word and thought, sign and meaning can never become one." See *Reading Deconstruction Deconstructive Reading* (Lexington: University Press of Kentucky, 1983), pp. 16–17.

8. Atkins explains the Derridean concept of deferral: "The possibility of the sign, substituting for the thing in a system of differences, thus depends upon deferral, that is putting off into the future any grasping of the 'thing itself.'" See *Reading*, p. 17.

9. Calderón, *El hijo del sol, Faetón*, in A. Valbuena Briones, ed. *Calderón de la Barca: Obras completas*, vol. 1 (Madrid: Aguilar, 1969), p. 1866, col. a. Because verses are not numbered, I have indicated the page and column (a or b) of the text. Quotations are from this edition of the play; English translations of the text are mine.

10. Terence Hawkes would define this function as an index. "In the index, the relationship is concrete, actual and usually of sequential causal kind. . . . Smoke is an index of fire." See *Structuralism and Semiotics* (Berkeley: University of California Press, 1977), p. 129.

11. I use the term *symbolically* here only in the semiotic sense. Hawkes explains that "In the symbol the relationship between signifier and signified is arbitrary; it requires the active presence of the interpretant to make the signifying connection." See *Structuralism and Semiotics*, p. 129.

12. Several Spanish dictionaries, *Diccionario de Autoridades*, *Diccionario de la Real Academia*, and *Barcía*, trace the figurative use of the word "reef" (escollo) in literature.

13. The extravagant stage settings of Calderón's mythological plays has been the subject of much favorable and unfavorable criticism. Some critics see it as superfluous visual fluff; others, as consummate integration of the visual and verbal texts. For a representative sampling of these disparate views see Marcelino Menéndez y Pelayo, *Calderón y su teatro* (Madrid: A. Pérez Dubrull, 1884); Ludwig Pfandl, *Historia de la literatura nacional española en la edad de oro*, trans. Jorge Rubio Balaguer (Barcelona: Sucesores de Juan Gili, 1933); N. D. Shergold, *A History of the Spanish Stage* (Oxford: Clarendon Press, 1967); and Sage, "The Function of Music."

14. Greene, "'Excellent Dumb Discourse,'" p. 196.

15. William Shakespeare, *The Tempest*, ed. Louis B. Wright, Folger edition (New York: Washington Square Press, 1966), 1.1.74–75. Further citations are from this edition.

16. Calderón's primary Spanish source of the Phaethon myth was probably Pérez de Moya's *Philosophia secreta*. Two articles that deal with Calderón's sources and adaptations are Pierre Paris, "La Mythologie de Calderón," in *Homenaje ofrecido a Menéndez Pidal* (Madrid: Editorial Hernando, 1925), pp. 557–70; and Margarita Gómez Mingorance, "Apolo y Climene. El hijo del sol, Faetón (Análisis de dos comedias calderonianas)," in *Actas del Congreso Internacional sobre Calderón y el teatro del Siglo de Oro*, vol. 1 (Madrid: CSIC, 1983), pp. 461–76.

17. The introduction of The Folger Library edition of *The Tempest*, and *Northrop Frye on Shakespeare* (New Haven: Yale University Press, 1986), pp. 173–74, contain further discussion of Shakespeare's sources.

18. Berger comments on this parallel in "Prospero's Art," p. 226.

19. R. S. White bases his analysis of *The Tempest* on this mythological presence in a

romance. The mixture of two modes, according to White, creates one of the basic tensions of the play: "There is an aloof classicism which pulls against the romance elements, imposing a sense of stasis upon a medium which . . . deals centrally with change and flux." See *Let Wonder Seem Familiar* (Atlantic Highlands, N.J.: Humanities Press, 1985), p. 159.

20. Several studies explore the exact nature of Prospero's magic. See Berger, "Prospero's Art"; Barbara L. Estrin, "Telling the Magician from the Magic in *The Tempest*," *Bucknell Review* 25 (1980): 170–87; and West, *Shakespeare & the Outer Mystery*, pp. 80–95.

# Translating Calderón: Some Problems
## Kenneth Muir

THERE are two legitimate aims in attempting the impossible task of translating poetic drama. The first is one that I followed in translating plays by Molière and Racine. Drama groups, dissatisfied with existing translations of plays they wished to put on, appealed to me as a member with some experience as a writer to provide better ones. G. Wilson Knight, my colleague at Leeds, wanted to produce *Athalie;* he knew I had translated some speeches of Racine to accompany records, and he urged me to attempt the whole play. His production was sufficiently successful for Eric Bentley to invite me to translate four other plays of Racine for Dramabooks.[1]

The second motive is the desire to extend the repertory of plays available in English. I felt particularly that there were absurdly few plays of the Golden Age of Spanish Drama, existing in actable translations, whereas in Germany seventy-four Calderón plays had been translated, most of them more than once.[2] There was, moreover, a fatal tendency for English translators to serve up yet another version of *La vida es sueño* or *El alcalde de Zalamea*.

Not wishing to compete with other translators, and having a particular admiration for the comedies, Ann L. Mackenzie and I avoided plays which had been done before, although it turned out that *El secreto a voces* had been translated in 1853 as *The Secret in Words* by Denis Florence MacCarthy and adapted by Robert Bridges under the title of *The Humours of the Court* (1893). William Wycherley, moreover, had used the plot of *Mañanas de abril y mayo* in his totally different *Love in a Wood*, where it is submerged in several other plots. The seven Calderón versions we have so far published are all comedies[3] and, like the two tragedies on which we are now engaged—*La cisma de Ingalaterra* and *El mayor monstruo los celos*[4]—though often discussed by the critics were not available in English. The work we have done on these nine plays has confronted us with numerous problems, some of them insoluble, and has compelled us to make interim decisions on policy.

The first problem which every translator must face is the difference between Spanish audiences in the seventeenth century and English or American audiences today. They differ in their beliefs, their prejudices, their codes of conduct, their expectations of drama and poetry. Many years ago I was introduced to E. V. Rieu, the general editor of the Penguin translations, who was looking for someone to translate Molière. He had heard of a production of *Le Misanthrope* by the York Settlement Community Players, in a translation by William Melton and myself, and he asked me the nature of the translation. I told him it was in prose—this was long before the brilliant verse translations of Wilbur and Harrison—and he said "Good!" Then I added: "I have tried to write it in the style of the late seventeenth century—as though I were a contemporary of Wycherley or Congreve." "Oh, no!" he said in horror, "we can't have that. We must be absolutely modern." I pointed out the dress, the customs and manners of the age of Louis XIV were so different from ours that a modern prose version would be completely at odds with the style and sentiments of the original, and that modern English audiences were perfectly at home with the style of Restoration comedy, captivated as they were by the acting of Edith Evans as Millamant, Lady Wishfort and Mrs. Sullen. I might have added, but tactfully refrained, that Mr. Rieu's own prose version of Homer, although a bestseller, gave one a somewhat inadequate idea of the original.

After nearly half a century I still believe that to be absolutely modern is a futile aim and that it nearly always means the elimination of the poetry without leading to a greater understanding of the play. It is argued that Calderón was modern to his original audiences, and that to conceal this fact by using less than modern diction is to give a totally false impression. But, as Thomas Gray said, "the language of the age is never the language of poetry," and Shakespeare with his inveterate coinages was as difficult in 1600 as he is today. The modernity of Calderón is similarly exaggerated. In our translations, therefore, we have used a language which would be understood by Dryden's contemporaries, though avoiding obvious anachronisms. Some archaic words are needed to convey seventeenth-century concepts. One reviewer complained that we had used words and idioms which were not in accordance with modern American usage. Although the translations were published in Kentucky, Ann L. Mackenzie comes from Scotland, and I come of Scottish descent. Apart from that we had made it clear that we had adopted a style nearer to the seventeenth century than to the twentieth, and nearer to that of York than that of New York. We felt that such a style, if successful, would mediate between the age of Calderón and that of Eliot and Pinter.

Some translators have been tempted to improve on the originals, as adaptors of Shakespeare in the late seventeenth century, such as Davenant and Tate, thought of ways of improving his masterpieces—*Macbeth* and *King Lear*. Posterity has not shared their optimism. One translator who thought he could improve on Calderón was Edward FitzGerald, whose most famous work was based on a poem by Omar Khayyam. He was not a dramatist in an age when even the best poets (Tennyson, Browning, Arnold) failed signally to write successful plays. Yet FitzGerald believed that Victorian taste was superior to that of the Golden Age. In his preface he explains the modifications he has introduced into his versions:

> I do not believe an exact translation of this poet can be very successful; retaining so much that, whether real or dramatic Spanish passion, is still bombast to English ears, and confounds otherwise distinct outlines of character; conceits that were a fashion of the day; or idioms that, true and intelligible to one nation, check the current of sympathy in others to which they are unfamiliar; violations of the probable, nay *possible,* that shock even healthy romantic licence; repetition of thoughts and images that Calderón used (and smiled at) as so much stage properties—so much, in short, that is not Calderón's own better self, but concession to private haste or public taste by one who so often relied upon some striking dramatic crisis for success with a not very accurate audience, and who, for whatever reason, was ever averse from any of his dramas being printed.[5]

Most of the "faults" FitzGerald ascribes to Calderón are equally apparent in Shakespeare—conceits, violations of the probable (e.g., the resurrection of Thaisa), repetition of thoughts and images, striking dramatic crises.[6] But FitzGerald, while claiming that he had retained the finer part of Calderón's plays, confessed that he had

> sunk, reduced, altered and replaced, much that seemed not; simplified some perplexities, and curtailed or omitted scenes that seemed to mar the breadth of general effect . . . and in some measure have tried to compensate for the fulness of sonorous Spanish, which Saxon English at least must forego, by a compression which has its own charm to Saxon ears.[7]

It is surely obvious that anyone who is so out of sympathy with the essential characteristics of Calderón's style ought to leave the task of translation to someone who admires it. Mirabel liked Millamant with her faults, liked her *for* her faults; and the ideal translator of Calderón should be similarly prejudiced in his favor.

The FitzGerald translations are mostly in blank verse, reasonably competent and fluent, but somewhat lacking in individuality. It has been filtered down from imitators of the lesser Elizabethan dramatists. The style is not varied to suit the different characters. One of his versions, *El alcalde de Zalamea,* is in prose. He argues that the first two acts consist of "homely talk," and that although Isabel's speech after her rape contains some of Calderón's finest poetry, he has deliberately made it prosaic to enable it to blend with the rest of the play. This perverse decision has disastrous results:

> Nunca amanezca a mis ojos
> la luz hermosa del día,
> porque a su sombra no tenga
> vergüenza yo de mí misma.
> ¡Oh tú, de tantas estrellas
> primavera fugitiva,
> no des lugar a la aurora,
> que tu azul campana pisa,
> para que con risa y llanto
> borre tu apacible vista!
> y ya que ha de ser, que sea
> con llanto, mas no con risa!
> Detente, oh mayor planeta,
> más tiempo en la espuma fría
> del mar; deja que una vez
> dilate la noche esquiva
> su trémulo imperio.[8]

> Oh never, never might the light of day arise and
> show me to myself in my shame! Oh, fleeting morning
> star, mightest thou never yield to the dawn that
> even now presses on thy azure skirts! And thou,
> great Orb of all, do thou stay down in the cold
> ocean foam; let night for once advance her
> trembling empire with thine!

The same passage is translated by Edwin Honig:

> Oh, never let the glorious day
> touch my eyes again nor waken me
> to know my shame beneath its shade!
> Oh morning star, harbinger of so
> many fleeting planets, stay and give
> no quarters to the dawn which now
> invades thy bluest canopy.
> Let it not erase thy quiet face
> with dewy smiles and tears.

> But I fear this must come to pass,
> admit no smile at all, dissolve
> in tears. Now, sun, thou greatest star
> of all, delay, hold back,
> and linger yet a while below
> in the ocean of cold foam.[9]

I shall discuss later Professor Honig's avowed aims in his translations. In this passage he uses assonance and concealed rhyme, presumably intentionally. Although it conveys something of Isabel's feelings and is free of verbiage, to my ear the verse is awkwardly irregular and flawed by three awkward enjambments. One is driven to ignore the line endings and read the lines as prose.

A third version of the same passage is that of Adrian Mitchell, written for a production in 1981. Mitchell translates Isabel's speech into regular four-stressed lines, knit together by the repetition of "light," "might," and "bright," and of the phrases "I never want" and "Just for this once."

> I never want to see the light,
> The lovely light ever again.
> I never want to see myself
> My shameful self, ever again
> Night sky, with your dark blue meadows,
> Bright with a million star-flowers,
> Don't let the dawn walk towards me
> With that young sunshine smile of hers.
> If you can't keep the dawn away
> Let her come with eyes full of rain.
> Not mocking me with laughing light.
> King of all planets, mighty Sun
> Just for this once, wait down below
> The cold sea a little longer.
> Just for this once let the shy night
> Rule her shining, trembling empire,
> A little longer hiding me.[10]

This strays too far from the original, and one could hardly guess from any of the three versions the poetical quality of that original. All three translators were poets, but only very occasionally has a good English poet suceeded in conveying a sense of Calderón's greatness. The best example is Shelley's free version of key scenes from *El mágico prodigioso*.

Apart from the poetical loss, these three versions of Isabel's soliloquy provide little help to the actress playing the role. She has to express the agony of the victim of rape while constrained by the formal beauty of the poetry. The combination of genuine feeling and poetic beauty was achieved by Shakespeare in the meditation of Lucrece after her rape; and, in drama, the wish to undo the past is hauntingly expressed by Thomas Heywood in *A Woman Killed with Kindness* when Frankford finds his wife in her lover's arms:

> Oh God, oh God, that it were possible
> To undo things done, to call back yesterday.
> That time could turn up his swift sandy glass,
> To untell the days, and to redeem these hours;
> Or that the sun
> Could rising from the West, draw his coach backward,
> Take from the account of time so many minutes,
> Till he had all these seasons called again,
> Those minutes and those actions done in them
> Even from her first offence, that I might take her
> As spotless as an angel in my arms.

Heywood is a minor dramatist, but in this speech he conveys better than any of Calderón's translators one aspect of Isabel's speech.

Elizabethan drama is written predominantly in blank verse, although there are many scenes in prose and some in rhyme. French classical drama is written almost exclusively in rhymed alexandrines. But, unlike the other two dramatic flowerings, the plays of the Spanish Golden Age have an extraordinary variety of poetic forms. In *El mayor monstruo los celos,* for example, Calderón uses nine different verse forms, including 16 ten-line stanzas, 67 five-line stanzas, and two sonnets, but most of the play is written in the *romance* form. *El mágico prodigioso* has a similar variety. One translator, Denis Florence MacCarthy, tried to preserve the Spanish verse forms in this and other plays, but the results are said to be unactable and unreadable. Professor Honig, acknowledging that this was so, felt that the usual resource of English translators, blank verse, was inevitably unsatisfactory because it was "lost in effect to the metronomic rhythms, diction and inversions of the seventeenth century."[11] To this it must be said that no good blank verse has metronomic rhythms, and it is possible to write blank verse without any of the characteristics Professor Honig deplores, as Shakespeare, Milton and Wordsworth, Keats and Shelley all demonstrated. He comes up with a different solution:

I use a syllabic line patterned on the octosyllabic *romance,* but different from its model (which sometimes omits and sometimes adds a syllable) in permitting a regular six-to-nine syllable limitation. The advantage of such flexibility is that the basic syllabic quantity allows for a fairly regular accentual beat to emerge in a variety of trimeter, tetrameter and pentameter lines that is not foreign to the English ear, and yet is just strange enough to suggest the Spanish norm.

Professor Honig is aware that some will object that his lines read like maladjusted prose: he points out that "there is the same effect in the originals when prose diction is cast in verse simply to abide by Golden Age conventions," and he hopes that his versions will be welcomed by those who dislike the insipidities, archaisms, and anachronisms inseparable from blank verse translations.

Professor Honig claims for himself an extraordinary metrical freedom, so large that one doubts whether the beat is "fairly regular," and whether the verse satisfies an English ear or suggests the Spanish norm. We may choose as an example of his method the speech in the last act of *La dama duende,* when the charming heroine confesses her love to the man she has tricked. Here one would expect not "prose diction cast in verse," but some of the best poetry:

> To love you
> I became a phantom in my own house.
> To honor you, I became
> the living tomb of my own secret.
> Indeed, I could not tell you that
> I loved you nor how much
> I respected you, for fear
> that any open declaration
> would jeopardize your presence
> as our guest, compelling you
> to quit the house at once.
> I only sought your favor
> because I loved you and because
> I feared to lose you. My only thought
> was keeping you to cherish
> and obey you all my life, to wed
> my soul with yours, and so all
> my desire was to serve you
> as now my plea is but
> to urge you to support me
> in my pressing need.[12]

I asked a group of graduates to read this passage and only one said anything in its favor. To most the lines seemed unmetrical and unscannable and not giving the impression of a young woman speaking. The division into lines is confusing because one can only read them as prose, prose, moreover, which is halting. A much more favorable example of Honig's method, because it can be read as verse, is Isabel's soliloquy, quoted above. My suspicion that some critics want verse to be read as prose was raised by a reviewer of *Four Comedies* who complained that I had printed each line with an initial capital. This, he said, was not merely contrary to Spanish custom but it prevented the lines from being read uninterruptedly (i.e., as prose).

The verse of Calderón is so different from that of any English dramatic verse that any attempt to copy it is bound to seem alien to an English audience. Even if a translator could be found to write ten-line stanzas as part of the dialogue while remaining faithful to the sense of the original, it would sound to playgoers more like a poetry recital than a play and they would cease to be interested either in the characters or in the action. Shakespeare does use a sonnet in *Romeo and Juliet,* sharing it between the lovers at their first meeting so as to suggest a marriage of true minds; and in *Hamlet, Othello,* and *All's Well that Ends Well* he uses rhymed couplets for particular purposes—for a play within a play, for satirical verses by Iago, and for Helena's hypnosis of the King.[13] But blank verse, nearer to prose but never identical with prose, was his usual medium. In listening to it, we are hardly conscious of the medium; we are listening to the characters.[14] This seems to me to be of fundamental importance. We do not want versions of foreign plays where the medium is more important than the meaning. T. S. Eliot was so depressed by the spectacle of culture vultures, piously bored in a good cause with the glazed look of people listening to poetry, that he expressed the hope that audiences would not recognize that his later plays were in verse. In some productions of Shakespeare, one can sense the embarrassment of some actors when they have to deliver rhymed verse—they hurry past the rhymes as though they were ashamed of them.[15] Some members of the audience shut off their attention when they hear rhyming. This is a pity, but it is something we must live with.

It means that in our time, and in Britain, blank verse and prose are the only acceptable media, and for poetic drama verse is obviously more suitable than prose.[16] It must not be obviously modern in style, nor too obviously archaic. It can use words which are no longer in common use, but only if they are perfectly intelligible to a modern audience. It must give the impression of people conversing, not of actors reciting, but it must also be capable of rising above the commonplace and prosaic so as to express passion and beauty.

It should be added that the translator should be able to differentiate between one character and another by style as well as content. This gift is comparatively rare even among successful dramatists. Shakespeare himself did not possess it when he began writing. Half the characters in *Henry VI* talk alike; but when he wrote *Romeo and Juliet,* all the main characters—the lovers, Mercutio, Tybalt, Capulet, the Nurse—are brilliantly distinguished. T. S. Eliot, on the other hand, when *The Elder Statesman* was in rehearsal, actually transferred lines from Charles to Monica and from Monica to Charles. He wasn't interested in them as characters but only as mouthpieces.

What I am implying is that a translator of plays ought to possess many of the qualities of a dramatist, and he is more likely to be successful if he has himself acted and knows the kind of verse which can be effectively delivered in a theater. Professor Bruce Wardropper's prose version of *El mágico prodigioso,* excellent as it is for reading and as an interpretation, could never serve as an acting text.[17]

One other point should be mentioned. Calderón's *graciosos* speak a kind of verse, but the back-chat in which they engage and the stories they tell could not be rendered in English verse. Although some of Shakespeare's early servants sometimes use rhyming doggerel, his later servants, along with rustics and comics, use only prose. The *graciosos* should speak prose as a matter of class distinction and as a suitable medium for their witticisms (except, of course, when they are parodying their masters' affectations). I have outlined some of the problems facing translators of poetic drama, but I need hardly say that I am not pretending that Ann L. Mackenzie and I have solved them, even to our own satisfaction. Some problems are unsolvable—what to do about puns, for example, and how to represent the jargon of the *précieuse* in *No hay burlas con el amor.*

## Notes

1. Jean Racine, *Five Plays,* trans. Kenneth Muir (New York: Hill and Wang, 1960).
2. See Henry W. Sullivan, *Calderón in the German Lands* (Cambridge: Cambridge University Press, 1983).
3. Pedro Calderón de la Barca, *Four Comedies,* trans. Kenneth Muir and Ann L. Mackenzie (Lexington: University of Kentucky Press, 1980).

4. To be published in bilingual editions by Aris and Phillips.

5. *Eight Dramas of Calderón,* trans. Edward FitzGerald (London: Macmillan, 1906), pp. 1–2.

6. Boris Pasternak, in translating Shakespeare, came to the conclusion that iterative imagery was a sign of haste and carelessness, not a subtle poetic and dramatic device.

7. FitzGerald, *Eight Dramas,* p. 2.

8. Ibid., p. 292.

9. Pedro Calderón de la Barca, *Four Plays,* trans. Edwin Honig (New York: Hill and Wang, 1961), p. 190.

10. Pedro Calderón de la Barca, *The Mayor of Zalamea,* trans. Adrian Mitchell (Edinburgh: Salamander Press, 1981).

11. Honig, *Four Plays,* p. xxv.

12. Ibid., p. 303.

13. *Romeo and Juliet* 1.5.88ff; *Hamlet* 3.2.150ff; *Othello* 2.1.129ff; *All's Well that Ends Well* 2.1.124–89.

14. After the Restoration the rhymed heroic play had a brief vogue, but the audiences were never absorbed in the action and Dryden tired of his "long-loved mistress rhyme." Wilbur and Harrison have shown that audiences can now enjoy rhymed couplets in translations of Molière, but I have yet to be convinced that they are happy with couplets in tragedy.

15. The same thing sometimes happens in modern productions of Racine.

16. It may well be true that in the United States blank verse is not so natural a medium. At least I have noticed that many good students in three or four American universities frequently fail to preserve the rhyme of Shakespeare's lines (e.g., by pronouncing Juliet with an accent on the last syllable).

17. Calderón de la Barca, *The Prodigious Magician,* trans. and ed. Bruce Wardropper (Potomac, Maryland: Studia Humanitatis, 1982).

# Afterword

Walter Cohen
*Cornell University*

THE years since 1985 have witnessed the emergence of a new field of study in North American literary criticism: comparative accounts of the Golden Age *comedia* and late Tudor and early Stuart drama. There have been conferences devoted to the topic, as well as at least three volumes.[1] Although some of the similarities between the two theaters addressed in these papers and publications have been familiar since the seventeenth century, I know of no previous book-length study of the matter on this continent. The sudden spurt of interest does not yet constitute a critical school or tradition, however. In *Renaissance Drama in England and Spain* John Loftis is unaware of my *Drama of a Nation*, and the other contributors to the present collection, their acknowledgments in footnotes notwithstanding, are neither influenced by nor openly opposed to these two earlier works.

Yet the concerns common to the various writers make it hard to reduce the phenomenon to temporal and geographical coincidence. Most obvious is the emphasis on the shared formal, often generic, features of English and Spanish drama, in the absence of influence by one theatrical tradition upon the other. Loftis plausibly concludes a primarily negative survey of the use made by English Renaissance playwrights of Spanish dramatic sources with suggestions for further research: "Let us direct our attention to the resemblances and also the differences. . . . Such subjects will be more rewarding than source-hunting."[2] He himself focuses on the history play and especially the national history play of the recent past; in the present volume romantic comedy, pastoral, and romance receive most of the attention; and my own study considers both historical and romantic forms, albeit more briefly.

The critics in this collection do not usually specify the impulses behind their enterprise, but a recurrent motive is to use the comparison with what in the United States (and England) is well known (the English playwrights, especially Shakespeare) in order to bring greater recognition and esteem to what is relatively unknown (*Siglo de Oro* theater). For example, Kenneth Muir justifies his translation of Calderón's comedies by a "desire to extend the repertory of plays available in English." One might ask, however, what the grounds are for assuming that Golden Age plays are in fact underrepresented in the English-language world, and particularly in North America. Any comparative study would give one answer: Lope, Tirso, Calderón, and their contemporaries are far better known in Germany, France, and almost certainly Italy and England as well, than they are in the United States. Yet independent of the unevenness of international reception, the historical trajectory of Spain itself provides an explanation for an additional and more general pattern of relative neglect. The social and economic backwardness of the country since the late seventeenth century, the intimations of which can be detected in the *comedia,* has meant that Hispanic literature and theater have long since ceased to have the prestige in Europe enjoyed by English, French, or German culture.

This second form of asymmetry has an important consequence for comparative work on English and Spanish Renaissance drama. Both scholarship and criticism are far more voluminous and far more advanced on England than on Spain. In trying to periodize the drama of late sixteenth- and early seventeenth-century England, I could rely with confidence on prior research; in attempting to do the same for the *Siglo de Oro* theater, I took educated guesses. More generally, critics have a tendency to apply to the superficially undifferentiated mass of *comedias* the often highly developed generic categories employed in analysis of plays by Shakespeare and his contemporaries. In this sense the distinction between well-known England and unknown Spain drawn above goes not just for the intended audience but for the state of scholarship itself as well.

Yet such considerations, however persuasive, do not really begin to account for the marked increase of interest in the topic here in recent years. Two highly speculative possibilities, the first involving Spain and the second the United States, are perhaps worth mentioning. First, the death of Franco and the subsequent collapse of his governmental system now make it easier *not* to see Golden Age Spanish absolutism as the authoritarian, anti-Semitic forerunner of modern fascism. Spain now seems to display some of the characteristic marks of western European history: like France and England it went through a stage of absolutist rule in the early modern period before emerging—though belatedly—as an industrial bourgeois democracy. Perhaps this political shift and the accompanying change in political perception has opened the way to comparative studies of the *comedia.* Meanwhile in the

United States the empire strikes back, with the continuing growth of the Hispanic-language population, especially in Florida and the southwest—regions that once belonged to the Spanish empire and that eventually fell victim to American imperial expansion. The growing bilingualism of the country, though its primary international pull is undoubtedly toward Latin America, may also be contributing to an increased interest in peninsular Spanish culture.

On the other hand, the three volumes comparing English and Spanish Renaissance drama differ strikingly in purpose and method—differences that may be approached by asking why one might be disturbed by the relative neglect of the *comedia*. The most obvious answer is that critics want to promote their area of professional specialization—an omnipresent impulse. More interesting are two other possibilities. The writer may have some broader aim in undertaking the comparison, an aim whose tendentiousness would seem to violate the specificity of the plays but that could be valuable in its insistence on something being at stake. For better or worse, my goal was to solve a historical problem (the reasons for the similarities between Spanish and English theater) from a methodolgical perspective (Marxism) that thereby obtained a reciprocal validation. In so doing I hoped to foster a radical, popular appropriation of the ostensibly "high" cultural past. In this volume theoretical motives sometimes come to the fore—there are deconstructive essays by William Blue and especially Denise DiPuccio, for example—but as in Loftis's study the raison d'être more often lies elsewhere.

The primary justification for the undertaking is the conviction that the plays of Lope and his contemporaries, like the plays of Shakespeare and *his* contemporaries, are simply great. Although the literary and dramatic canon—its particular texts, principles of inclusion and exclusion, process of formation, and very existence—has come under skeptical scrutiny recently, canonicity is not a category that can be lightly dismissed. But often there is perhaps too easy an assumption of greatness, an assumption, moreover, that involves the invocation of Shakespeare as a norm. Edward Friedman's remarks on Rojas Zorrilla's *Los bandos de Verona* are a notable exception, and DiPuccio is surely right in attempting to define the criteria that earn the playwrights—in her case, Calderón and Shakespeare—canonical status.

If a critic takes canonicity for granted, a common result is an identification with the playwrights and plays. In a traditional literary historian like Loftis, this has mixed results. An appreciation of the national history play in the two countries produces a salutary focus on a genre that is distinctive, indeed almost unique, to England and Spain during the Renaissance. The resulting erudition will undoubtedly place future researchers in Loftis's debt. But the orientation toward topical plays that treat the rivalry between the two powers brings together national with foreign history plays, effectively weakening the generic point with little compensatory comparative ideological analysis of nationalism, xenophobia, religious chauvinism, or the like.

In a discussion of drama about military campaigns led by members of the high aristocracy and about the national and international political affairs of the monarchy, this latter lack has the troubling consequence of identifying the author, as an enthusiastic proponent of the plays, with the ruling class and hence with militarism, imperialism, racism, and genocide. And this is so even though Loftis acknowledges the misery that resulted from English and especially Spanish policies. Thus, to take only one of many possible examples, he defends Lope's *El Brasil restituido* from charges of anachronistic bravado on the grounds that when it was composed in 1625 it was still plausible to be optimistic about Spain's international prowess.[3] But this play concerns the question of whether the Spanish or the Dutch will exploit the indigenous population of America. Here, then, the limitations of an uncritical, old historicist appreciation of the canon come clearly into view.

In the present volume appreciation of canonical works has more typical consequences. Most of the essays collected here are broadly speaking formalist accounts. The purpose of the volume—comparative studies of Shakespeare and the *comedia*—encourages intrinsic criticism specifically designed to reveal similarities between an English and a Spanish play. The relative lack of primary research follows from this focus. It is hard enough to carry out such an investigation in a single field, and far more difficult to work in this fashion in two different languages simultaneously. Nonetheless, Loftis's book and Bruce Golden's essay demonstrate that the undertaking is not impossible.

The comparative readings are shaped by the assumption of canonicity in still more particular ways. Although the dramatic text is rightly assumed to be the result of, among other things, an authorial intention, problems arise when most or all textual features considered significant are traced back to the purposeful playwright. This practice can blunt the critical edge of the innovative strategies often employed in the collection, especially deconstruction and intertextuality. Writing of *The Tempest* and Calderón's *El hijo del sol, Faetón,* DiPuccio concludes: "the unresolved tension of both plays centers on whether or not the characters will be able to define strange events that puzzle them. Two dramatic geniuses have earned the critical right to ask this question. Long literary careers awakened their sensitivity to the advantages and drawbacks of linguistic command. . . . Two seventeenth-century artistic works preempt twentieth-century critical trends to dismantle logic in the text. They lay bare examples of the arbitrary nature of language and its effects on comprehension of cosmic harmony." Evidently the sentences that come before the ellipsis stress the deliberate act of creativity; those that follow it, though drawn from the same paragraph, emphasize the impersonal fact of creation. We therefore cannot know for sure whether the dramatists deliberately foreground "the arbitrary nature of language" or whether, to take the somewhat less likely inference, their texts do so against the playwrights' ostensible intention of celebrating a comprehensible "cosmic harmony."

The essays interested in intertextuality clearly stress intentionality. In an account of Calderón's *Mañana será otro día,* Blue notes the distancing effect produced by "the manipulating hand of the dramatist. . . . The playwright uses self-conscious intertextuality as well to achieve similar effects." Frederick de Armas deplores the lack of research on "intertextual questions" in the study of *As You Like It* and then immediately proceeds to invoke as an important exception Douglas Bush's "pioneering work on mythology in Shakespeare." Friedman looks at Lope's *Castelvines y Monteses* and Rojas Zorrilla's *Los bandos de Verona,* both of them based on the same Italian models as *Romeo and Juliet* but characterized by a "particular deviation from the source material": the substitution of a happy ending. "The happy ending is, at the same time, a dramatic convention and an intertextual counterconvention; it follows Spanish Golden Age drama's resistance to tragedy in breaking with the denouement of the narratives from which it derives." In each of these essays intertextuality refers primarily to the playwright's conscious use of literary, high-cultural sources and allusions, rather than to the way the text and performance are informed by a multiplicity of codes—that may or may not be literary, that the dramatist may or may not be aware of, and that may or may not be a matter of real authorial choice. One sees here, then, a common circumscribing of intertextuality, a limitation of the area of inquiry to the terrain of intellectual and literary history.

The canonical orientation of the volume is most evident, however, in the normative treatment of Shakespeare. It is not just that Shakespeare's stature is unquestioned; it is, rather, that a particular interpretation of Shakespeare is often taken for granted. In such cases Shakespeare becomes an uncontroversial standard against which the Spanish playwrights can be measured. Most of the essays—de Armas's is a partial exception—therefore have more original things to say about the *comedia* than about the most famous English drama contemporary with it. Even those pieces that draw extensively on recent Shakespeare studies do not always register the existence of a contemporary critical debate. Except perhaps for Blue's essay, they generally ignore what I take to be the most important and controversial development of the present decade: the rise of political criticism and particularly of Marxism, feminism, and new historicism.[4] The limited amount of Marxist writing cited is usually invoked in the service of deconstruction. The very large body of feminist criticism of Shakespeare is rarely mentioned, though it is fair to add that Golden's essay addresses similar concerns. And new historicist studies such as the work of Stephen Greenblatt, currently the most influential critic of Renaissance English literature and theater, are simply invisible.[5] This volume also steers clear of political approaches to Golden Age literature and theater, whether by Américo Castro, Noël Salomon, José Antonio Maravall, José María Díez Borque, John Beverly, or the international cast of contributors in Wlad Godzich and Nicholas Spadaccini's recent collection.[6] No doubt partly because of my own critical orientation, I find these omissions regrettable.

Another way of registering the distance from politics is to return to the generic predilection noted earlier—the focus on romantic comedy, pastoral, and romance. Such a choice makes it easier *not* to address political questions than would be possible if the national history play were emphasized as in Loftis's study. The neglect of this genre is unfortunate for the reason given above: it is the one dramatic form that separates England and Spain collectively from the rest of Renaissance Europe. The more comic genres, belonging as they do to a general, international practice pioneered on the sixteenth-century Italian stage, possess no equivalent distinctiveness. In this instance, then, fully adequate comparative studies would have to be at least trinational.

The formalist approach to the canon common to this volume arises, it seems to me, from the particular heritage of *comedia* studies. I am referring to the important work of the British Hispanists, who in many respects dominated the field from the

1930s until very recently. Their continuing influence, as it manifests itself in the current collection, may be observed in the formalist orientation, in the preference for Calderón and his school to Lope and *his* school, and in the corresponding attention to the relationship between the theater and the court. This latter interest is shared by new historicist critics of Shakespeare, but the relationship is usually treated in a more demystifying fashion than one finds here. Failure to adopt some such skeptical stance can produce the kind of identification with royal power noticed earlier in Loftis's book. At the very least it has the unintended consequence of seeming to ratify an elitist view of art.

Yet the preceding comments on the other essays in this collection are surely one-sided. For they exclude any reckoning of the specific situation, shared purpose, positive logic, or significant contribution of the volume. I am referring not to consistent, programmatic statements but to a general, sometimes implicit sense of direction shared by these articles, despite their evident heterogeneity. The underlying rationale of this volume is a settling of accounts with the prior generation of critics of the *comedia*, and especially with the British Calderonistas. If this view is correct—and it must be admitted that none of the contributors explicitly makes this claim—some of my earlier comments acquire a different resonance. The discussions of Shakespeare reveal themselves less as ends than as means. The same goes for the use of criticism of Shakespeare. For the purposes of comparison with the *comedia*, it matters little which approach to the English playwright informs the discussion. In referring above to a normative view of Shakespeare, I tried to remain at a fairly high level of generality in order to imply that any canonical treatment of the dramatist could easily limit, and often conservatively limit, criticism. Yet whatever the ideological baggage the name of Shakespeare drags along behind it, the result remains fresh in the context of the reception of Golden Age theater.

It may be worth looking at the particular pattern of originality in some detail. Susan Fischer's essay neatly illustrates the different temporalities of Shakespeare studies and *comedia* studies. The reliance on Frye and Barber seems to me genuinely useful in the ensuing discussion of *El vergonzoso en palacio*. We all know that a methodology long established in one discipline can have a remarkable cutting edge when transferred to another. It is important to recognize that a similar principle operates in the movement across fields within a single discipline. In a somewhat more polemical though nonetheless cautious fashion, Friedman takes his distance from a central position of the leading English scholar A. A. Parker: "It is possible that Lope's concept of tragicomedy does not rely as heavily as Parker would have it on poetic justice as a moral criterion." Blue is more explicit in criticizing perhaps the most important American counterpart of the British Hispanists: "Arnold Reichenberger once said that in these plays it does not matter if a woman gets the man she wants as long as she gets a man. But that simply is not true, and *Mañana será otro día* takes great pains to criticize arranged or forced marriages by fathers (or, I will add, by dramatists)."

Such comments suggest the nature of the critique launched against the previous generation and the new view of the *comedia* that begins to emerge. Opposing the traditional assumption of the formal, moral, and metaphysical closure of Golden Age drama, the contributors to this collection emphasize openendedness and subversion, important dimensions of the plays that have been systematically occluded. It is in this context that the recourse to Shakespeare and to Shakespeare studies acquires its rationale. For although Shakespeare and his theater have often been put to conservative uses, they have regularly been available as well for more progressive appropriation in both aesthetic and political terms. At least implicit recognition of this possibility informs most of the essays collected here.

The results are evident in the rhetoric of the critics. Golden concludes, "Calderón and Shakespeare are using certain dominant social and cultural codes analogously. They neither approve nor condemn popular belief in these codes; instead they put the codes to the test in the popular drama, showing the effect that the codes have on action and character. They, like all great writers, leave it to their audience to determine whatever significance there may be in all of this." Fischer ends similarly: "By so encouraging the search for multiplicity of meaning, these Shakespearean and Tirsian texts defy being reduced to a set of monolithic structures based on the spectator's, the reader's, the critic's, or the author's preconceived notion of life and love." For Friedman "the brush with tragedy does not have the same impact in *Los bandos de Verona* that it has in *Castelvines y Monteses*. The retelling distorts the focus, and tragicomedy leads not to delightful variation but to mixed messages." "Both *El ganso de oro* and *As You Like It* are about breaking boundaries," according to de Armas.

I have already cited some of DiPuccio's remarks along these lines. Here is another characteristic formulation: "Two conflictive arguments, then, undermine each other throughout the plays:

language leads to cosmic awareness; the arbitrary and deficient nature of language precludes that outcome." In an essay whose combination of linguistic and social sensitivity I find particularly congenial, Blue argues that "Comedy, like carnival, seems to offer up alternatives and then back away from them, but the possibilities, along with the doubts, fears, questions, and criticisms raised by these plays do not vanish when man marries woman in the last scene." And even Kenneth Muir, whose concern with translation points him almost in the opposite direction, concludes with what in this context is a symptomatically telling concession: "Some problems are unsolvable—what to do about puns, for example, and how to represent the jargon of the *précieuse* in *No hay burlas con el amor*."

These statements and many others that could be adduced help explain the significance of the deconstructive strategies employed in some of the essays. Those strategies are of course central to DiPuccio's argument. But they are also important for Blue—"What comedy questions, inverts, and destabilizes with its wordplay, with words 'grown so false,' is the ordered state itself"—and to a lesser extent for Fischer: "There is no 'simple antithesis' in *As You Like It*, for binary oppositions are continually modified or 'deconstructed,' and the same would apply to *El vergonzoso*." In the context of *comedia* studies, then, deconstruction almost inevitably acquires a more powerful political charge than is sometimes the case in fields that have historically been more open.

Finally, the essays in this volume suggest some of the useful directions further research might take. The effort to transform the field of *comedia* studies needs to be supplemented by a more systematic investigation of how that field can contribute to broader work on literature and theater. An obvious place to begin is the very point where this volume is located: comparative studies with Shakespeare. For if I am right in arguing that Shakespeare functions in these essays as a critical tool that can be brought to bear on the *comedia*, it seems only reasonable that the opposite procedure might produce useful results. The aim here would be to defamiliarize Shakespeare's plays by placing them in what remains a largely alien context in this country. Such an enterprise might contribute more generally to comparative literature studies, an area that came to special prominence during the 1970s through the writings of important theorists like Paul de Man and Fredric Jameson but that today seems to lack any clear sense of purpose. One possible approach is to work against the superficial cosmopolitanism but actually fundamental elitist ethnocentrism of a discipline that has traditionally privileged English, French, and German literatures at the expense of all others. In the transformation of comparative literature into world literature, a transformation that has enormous ideological complications but that could contribute to the ongoing struggle against racism and national chauvinism, students of the *comedia* have a modest but real role to play.

## Notes

1. Walter Cohen, *Drama of a Nation: Public Theater in Renaissance England and Spain* (Ithaca: Cornell University Press, 1985); John Loftis, *Renaissance Drama in England and Spain: Topical Allusion and History Plays* (Princeton: Princeton University Press, 1987); and the present collection. An additional volume may result from the papers presented at a conference entitled "Parallel Lives: English and Spanish National Drama, 1580–1680," at the University of Calgary in October 1987.

2. Loftis, *Renaissance Drama*, pp. 261–62.

3. Ibid., pp. 203–4.

4. For a survey of this criticism see Cohen, "Political Criticism of Shakespeare," in *Shakespeare Reproduced: The Text in History and Ideology*, ed. Jean E. Howard and Marion F. O'Connor (London: Methuen, 1987), pp. 18–46.

5. Stephen Greenblatt, *Renaissance Self-Fashioning: From More to Shakespeare* (Chicago: University of Chicago Press, 1980); Greenblatt, *Shakespearean Negotiations* (Berkeley: University of California Press, 1988).

6. Américo Castro, *De la edad conflictiva*, 2d ed. (Madrid: Taurus, 1963); Noël Salomon, *Recherches sur le thème paysan dans la comedia au temps de Lope de Vega* (Bordeaux: Féret, 1965); José Antonio Maravall, *Teatro y literatura en la sociedad barroca* (Madrid: Seminario y Ediciones, 1972); Maravall, *Culture of the Baroque: Analysis of a Historical Structure*, trans. Terry Cochran (Minneapolis: University of Minnesota Press, 1986); José María Díez Borque, *Sociología de la comedia española del siglo XVII* (Madrid: Cátedra, 1976); Díez Borque, *Sociedad y teatro en la España de Lope de Vega* (Barcelona: Bosch, 1978); John Beverly, *Aspects of Góngora's* Soledades (Amsterdam: Benjamins, 1980); Wlad Godzich and Nicholas Spadaccini, eds., *Literature among Discourses: The Spanish Golden Age* (Minneapolis: University of Minnesota Press, 1986).